The Hospitality Ladder

A No-BS Guide to Building Success in Customer
Service, and Life, from the Bottom Rung

A Motivational Book by Antoni L. Konecne

The Hospitality Ladder
A No-BS Guide to Building Success in Customer Service, and Life, from the Bottom Rung
© 2014 Antoni L. Konecne

The author is available for speaking engagements or consultation services. Send inquiries by email to: thehospitalityladder@gmail.com

Disclaimer: The author is a restaurant manager, not a scientist, doctor, or psychiatrist; although his wife tells him he is very handsome. The stories within this book are a representation of some of the observations, successes and failures of the author, and lessons learned from each experience. All accounts are accurate and true to the best of the author's knowledge and recollection, and as wild as some of the stories may seem, very little artistic license has been used. Effort has been taken to remove any identifying information from anecdotes to protect the identity of people who the stories are about. There exists no easy path to success and a person must work hard to get ahead in life. The author makes no guarantees or promises whatsoever in regards to the outcome of your efforts or as a result of reading this book. Direction, hard work, dedication, and drive, however, have worked quite well for the author, and many, many other people.

ISBN-13: 978-1505204261
ISBN-10: 1505204267

This book is dedicated to my wife Abby who has been the most loving, encouraging, kind, and understanding partner a restaurant manager could ever hope to have; to my Grandma for never giving up on me, and forcing me to believe I could do anything if I would just set my mind to it; my Mom for teaching me to be tough and resilient; my Grandpa for my work ethic and teaching me what true patience really is; my Dad for teaching me to stand up and fight; and, to my kids Kyle, Tara, Noah, and Sola Jayne for teaching me how true love can be. Thank you all for these—and so much more.

In Memory of my Grandma Mary. One of the toughest and most loving women I will ever know.

"Boys without scars don't have any cool stories to tell"

Table of Contents

Introduction   1

The Transformation   22

PART ONE—ATTITUDE

Chapter One—First, Love it!   30

Chapter Two—Understand the Passion   42

Chapter Three—The Hard Truth   47

Chapter Four—Understand Yourself   50

Chapter Five—Practice What You Preach   55

Chapter Six—Professionalism and Etiquette   59

Chapter Seven—Change Your Preposition   65

Chapter Eight—Flies and Honey   73

Chapter Nine—Don't Be (Deliberately) Obtuse   78

Chapter Ten—Choose Your Blood Type, B+ or B-   81

PART TWO--APTITUDE

Chapter Eleven—The "How-to" Rule of Tools and Self-Development   92

Chapter Twelve—Organization and Time Management   96

Chapter Thirteen—Feed Your Egg: A Trick to Help With Solution Based Thinking   101

Chapter Fourteen—Goal Setting   108

Chapter Fifteen—Get it Done…Now!   114

Chapter Sixteen—Teamwork   117

Chapter Seventeen—Product Excellence   121

Chapter Eighteen—Training and Development   123

Chapter Nineteen—Your Boss's Job   128

Chapter Twenty—Suck it Up: Follow Loyally When   131
You Get Passed Up

PART THREE--ALTITUDE
Chapter Twenty-One—The Hospitality Ladder   136
Chapter Twenty-Two—The Shark Theory   148
Chapter Twenty-Three—"Ben" Service and Sales   151
Building
Chapter Twenty-Four—No Man's Land: Leading   161
without a Title
Chapter Twenty-Five—The Mysteries of the P&L   165
Chapter Twenty-Six—Some Notes on Cost Control   169
Chapter Twenty-Seven—Dealing With Theft   177
Chapter Twenty-Eight—Creating the Matrix: Staying   180
Compliant
Chapter Twenty-Nine—Fraternization   183
Chapter Thirty—Congratulations! You Asked   187
For It.

PART FOUR--FORTITUDE
Chapter Thirty-One—Your Salary   198
Chapter Thirty-Two—Recruiting, Interviewing, and   201
Hiring
Chapter Thirty-Three—How Much Would You Pay for   211
an Empty Chair?
Chapter Thirty-Four—Make it Fun! (Or Hire Someone   217
Who Can)
Chapter Thirty-Five—Feedback   219
Chapter Thirty-Six—Managing Conflict   224
Chapter Thirty-Seven—Crisis Management   229
Chapter Thirty-Eight—Guest Recovery   235

Chapter Thirty-Nine—Firing Your Guest   243
Chapter Forty—Ownership   251

Putting it All Together   258
Resources   262

INTRODUCTION

I have often wondered; at what point a person's experience, or ego, finally culminates in the decision to write a book? After all, I suppose it could be considered a feat of arrogance in some ways. What makes me the expert?

Well, to begin with, it's not about ego for me. Quite the contrary, the motivation to sit down and write this book really originated from a deep desire to understand what my experience really looks like—and, to better shape that experience to be a more effective leader. This work comes from a sincere desire to help and to understand.

If you have been gracious enough to open this book, then you are probably like me—you have a true desire to understand and improve yourself. If through my mistakes (Lord knows I have made my share—and then some), challenges and experience I can help you with that, then we are both better off.

Having managed hundreds, maybe thousands, of team members over the course of my career, I have learned a thing or two about people. One of the things I have learned is that most people want to do a good job and want to enjoy what they do. Second, I have found that too often we complicate things and make our own success more difficult than it needs to be.

I have also learned that my style isn't for everyone. Learning that has really helped me focus my energy and be more productive. My goal with this book is to give you a simple, no BS guide to becoming a better team member, manager, or owner through my extensive experience, successes, and failures—both as a lifelong professional in the hospitality industry, a person who is very passionate about self learning and development. I hope that my experience, my successes, and my mistakes can help you focus your energy, and ultimately become a more productive person, both at work and in life.

My journey has not been an easy one; and it is far from over. I make mistakes every day. I fail to heed my own advice from time to time. Stress and frustration get the better of me once in a while. I struggle day to day with some of the same things that you face, and I have successfully struggled through some of the same roadblocks some of you may be facing now.

In short, I am not perfect. And, surprise! Neither are you. We have to understand that about ourselves, and accept it. We have to learn to forgive ourselves when we do make mistakes, and not get so bogged down in guilt or the "woulda, coulda, shoulda" mentality. We have to learn from our mistakes and move on, and work tirelessly not to repeat them. And, if you do repeat the same mistakes, learn to forgive yourself. You'd forgive your children or your friends for the same thing right? So, why not treat yourself with the same courtesy and respect?

My work ethic developed at a very young age as I spent time with my Grandpa. I was raised poor and I grew up raising cattle and working on a farm. When we were happy and all was right with the world, we worked. When it was cold, we worked. When we were sick, we worked. When we were sad, we worked.

I am blue collar at the core and I believe in the power of hard work and tenacity. I believe that this country was founded on these principles and that a fundamental and frightening problem with The United States today is that we progressively and systematically, in my opinion, stray farther and farther from self-accountability and work ethic. I believe that these principles are *critical* to individual success, and that anything less is weakness.

Not-so-deep-down, I believe that people should be like me and those I grew up with. Fundamentally, I know that is not the case and it is possibly (but probably not) unreasonable to expect, and I have a real problem with the gap. And you should too, especially if you find yourself on the low end of it.

If you master the gap in work ethic, especially in this day and age, you will always be among the best people in any room. I do not expect perfection; I have made a ton of bad and impulsive decisions. I make mistakes every day. And, I respect courage, durability and hard work. While I have reaped many rewards along the way, I have also suffered some heavy costs.

This isn't a book for executives. It isn't a book for managers who already have the basics figured out, or people who are happy and successful where they are. It's not a book for owners who are running a successful business.

This is a book for people who are at the beginning of their careers. It is for the minimum wage workers who know there is more to life and all they need is just a little direction and encouragement. This book is for people who feel that they can't seem to get ahead or are stagnant where they are. This book is for the ambitious soldier who might never have had a general to teach them how to get to the next level. This is for the person who doesn't want to keep applying for the same low wage jobs year after year and wants to achieve a higher level of success for their family and for themselves.

This book isn't about me, it's about you and helping you learn to remove your own roadblocks and get on with your life and career. I will warn you, nothing in this book is easy. There are no get rich quick schemes in here and I am not going to burn pounds of body fat off of you in five days with a miracle pill. True self-reflection and self-improvement is some of the hardest work you will ever do. It takes immense courage, and it takes 100% commitment on your part and the drive and determination to back it up. If you are down with that, let's rock and roll. If you aren't sure, keep reading. Hopefully we can make you sure by the end of the last page.

Some people need back story and credentials, if that is you, then here you go. If that is not you, then feel free to jump to Chapter One. Like I stated before, I am a meat and potatoes guy, so to be honest with you, I probably would have made that jump a few sentences ago.

Currently, I serve as General Manager for a premium casual dining concept in Davenport, IA. My management career started a little over fifteen years ago. I have been a General Manager for three different businesses and have recognized a high level of success at each.

At this point, I am forty-one years old, and I have been in the hospitality industry for over twenty-six years. I have held and been successful at almost every single position in the restaurant, and bar and nightclub industries. I started in this business as a busboy and dish guy for a local steak house in Lenox, Iowa in 1989 and I have been a restaurant manager since 1999, when I started with a world famous chain as their service and bar manager. In short, I started as a busboy and worked my way up.

What I have learned to get me to this level can be beneficial to those striving for it.

As a boy, I grew up in a small Southwest Iowa town. I had a great childhood in a lot of ways, and I think like most kids, it was pretty terrible in a lot of ways too. My family is awesome, though, which makes the hard times easier to deal with. My mother has always been there for me through thick and through thin, and I have been blessed with a lot of great and supportive people in my family. In that sense I have been very lucky. Many of you reading this book don't have that level of support. That means your fight will be harder in many ways, but that's okay. The harder the fight, the sweeter the victory.

In Fourth Grade, I was diagnosed with ADHD (way before it was cool, by the way) and prescribed a popular brand name drug. I will never forget the terrible feeling that drug gave me. As an adult, I still seem to feel the lingering effects! I felt weird and emotional, and trapped. I remember asking my Mom to please let me stop taking it. She agreed without hesitation and, for better or worse, I embarked on the journey of managing this disorder myself. It has served me well in the restaurant business, but it has not been without some strife. Impulse control can be an issue with ADHD, and brother let me tell you…let's just say "The Adventures of Tony's Brain and Poor Decisions" could be a bestselling book of its own!

Psychologically speaking, I suffered through some pretty traumatic experiences as a young person. As youthful experiences do, these things shaped me and how I interact with the world. There are a lot of people out there who have had things *way* worse than I ever did, but I think it is important, for the purpose of this book, to understand some of the things that I have struggled through, and how I overcame the challenges in my life, both self-imposed and otherwise.

When I was very young, from eight to ten years old, I was a victim of systematic and prolonged sexual abuse at the hands of a male babysitter. When I was in sixth grade, my parents got divorced. The two years following that were absolutely terrible.

There were late night fights, and screaming matches, suicide attempts and broken doors, picture frames, fear and sadness. My sister and I would sit at the top of the stairs in secrecy and terror, praying for any escape. I remember being terrified a lot in those days.

One day, In the midst of my parent's divorce, a kid a grade below me tried to hit me in the head with a brick as I walked home from school. I turned around and broke his nose. He called his cousin who was in high school at the time, who came with a gang of older boys to intimidate me. He made a lot of noise, but he knew that being much older than me, if he touched me, he'd likely go to jail.

7

About a week later, my best friend since we were toddlers walked me home from school. Once we got to my front yard, he turned around and punched me in the face. He proceeded to beat the shit out of me. I later found out that the older cousin of the kid I punched had paid my friend fifteen bucks to exact revenge on me. I was absolutely crushed.

My adoptive father moved us around a lot when I was young. Looking back, I consider this a blessing and a curse. On one hand, I easily adapt to new environments and know how to make friends very quickly. These are valuable traits in any business, and have served me well in hospitality.

On the other hand, I tend not to get attached very easily and it can be difficult for me to form long lasting and deeply meaningful relationships. Also, it can be very easy for me to let go and walk away from something, since I do not fear striking out on my own or the "next thing". This isn't always a bad thing, but I have always regretted that I don't have any true lifelong friends.

From fourth grade to seventh grade, I moved five times and attended four different schools (one of them twice). At the last school we moved to (immediately following the revenge incident), in seventh grade I became a victim of severe bullying that was prolonged over a period of five years until the end of my junior year.

By severe, I can safely and conservatively estimate that I was punched at least once a day during the school year by someone much larger than me as hard as they could hit me for nearly the entire five years. Frequently, I would be held by one or more boys while several of them took turns punching me. Sometimes it was a full on beating, sometimes threats and name calling, sometimes a random sneak attack in the hallway, restroom, gym, or locker room. A favorite move was to sneak up behind me while I was taking a leak in the boy's room and shove me into the urinal as hard as they could.

I was small and weird in those days and I also received a seemingly endless tirade of vicious verbal taunting and abuse from my school mates.

Faggot. Geek. Pussy. These were some of my nicknames through high school.

I was too scared to fight, and I didn't want to. I wanted to play. I wanted to climb trees. I wanted to write poems and draw and talk to pretty girls and laugh and ride bikes and listen to music. I wanted to be nice to people, and I wanted people to be nice to me. Instead, I spent most of my days at school highly alert and defensive—and pretty much scared shitless.

Refusing to let the bullying hold me back, I still did things like run track and play baseball. I really wanted to fit in, and didn't want to be afraid, so I faked it a lot and tried to go about my school business as if nothing was wrong. I was never very good at sports, so this did not help. I also took a lot of home economics, and choir, band, drama and art classes which, in those days probably painted a bigger target on my back, but I enjoyed those things. And, it did help me make a few pretty good friends which made daily life tolerable.

Even though I felt like a coward most of the time, and I had not an iota of self confidence, powering through this time of my life taught me courage in the face of adversity and toughness. To this day it takes a lot of bad stuff to hold me back or even slow me down.

Death began to creep in. In a span of about twelve months through my sophomore and junior years in high school, one of my ex-girlfriends was brutally raped and murdered by an older man. Another close group of friends was killed in a tragic head on collision by a drunk running from the cops. My then girlfriend and I took this particularly hard because we had introduced our two friends who had begun dating. The girl's mother was driving my friend back to Villisca, Iowa when the accident took place.

Then, a classmate of mine committed suicide. The story was that he and some other boys had gotten caught vandalizing the school. After what must have been a pretty bad night, he locked himself in his bedroom and put a shotgun in his mouth. He and I had lockers next to one another since seventh grade, and weren't what I would call close friends, but friends just the same.

10

Suicide is never an easy thing to accept, and when you are young it can be very devastating and confusing. Our entire town was shocked. He was loved by all that knew him, and it was a very strange and scary time for those of us in his class, and I can only imagine how horrible it was for his family and closest friends.

It was around this same time that I started losing close family members. Up to then, I had a small handful of distant relatives die, but my Great Grandma Johnston was the first devastating loss. I loved her so much. She was a very small woman and loved candy! It turns out that she was diabetic and actually needed candy. Either way, I blame her for my acute addiction to chocolate!

Grandma Johnston's death was hard on me for many reasons; but the day she died, I had gone to my first rock concert in Des Moines, and had put off going to see her in the hospital. When I got home and heard the news, I pretty much lost it. I am not sure how other people really deal with death, but I really began to have problems with mortality. Death became so scary for me, to the point that I still spend a good deal of time worrying about it.

Early in high school my Mom married my stepdad. I call him Dad today. We definitely had our bouts at first and he did not start out as a very positive influence in my life, but as I got used to the idea of having a Dad in my life, and he got used to having kids in his, he really taught me a lot about being a man in general, including the importance of standing up for myself.

Finally, I did stand up for myself at the end of my junior year and came out on top. After that, the bullying tapered off. But also after that, I became a bully myself, which I feel guilty and hypocritical for to this day.

Not all of my youth was bad. In fact, a lot of it was really great! I have a ton of fond childhood memories of my Mom and Grandparents, my cousins and my sisters and little brother. I remember lots of really fun family vacations, trips to World's of Fun, and summers working on the farm.

As I became skilled at compartmentalizing the different pieces of my life, I could leave school and put all of the bad things in a basket, take a nap and wake up feeling pretty good about life. After that, it was okay to have fun. It was okay to laugh and sing, write and draw, and ride bikes and hike through the woods. I could tune out the bad to find solace in the good.

Family has always been my number one, and for all of the screwed up things that happened to me when I was a kid, my family has always been a powerfully positive force. I loved working with my Grandpa and visiting my grandparents in the summers, weekends, and winter breaks. School was so terrible that I learned to really dive into work.

One of my first jobs when I was in high school was at Cheese's Grocery Store in Lenox, Iowa. I loved it. I worked with my best friend and I made three dollars and thirty-three cents per hour.

One of our jobs in those days was to physically count the empty beer and soda cans that people would drop off in huge garbage bags. In Iowa, each can is worth five cents, and there was no such thing as a big machine that gobbles up the cans and dispenses a ticket for the amount of the deposit. No, we had to do it by hand; and, somehow, I always seemed to get the bag that someone had thrown a dirty diaper or some other foul thing into.

Please spare yourself your own research on this, there is nothing quite like sorting through hundreds of stale beer cans that have been marinating in puke and dirty diapers for weeks in the stagnant summer heat of an old dirty garage.

Toward the end of high school and into college, I really started building my own roadblocks. I mean I had crews working around the clock, three shifts a day building these things. I started drinking and smoking at pretty young age. In college I got my first taste of popularity, and I liked the taste! I went to class about twice in three years, became a lead singer in a popular cover band, fought a lot, broke things, and drank unbelievable quantities of alcohol. Excess was my way of coping with my past, and I didn't realize it, but I was really hanging on to all of the anger I had built up since childhood. Direction was something I knew nothing about.

I dodged a ton of bullets. The fact I am alive to write this book is a flat out miracle. Don't try any of what I am about to discuss, please—*especially* if you are one of my kids. To show off, I used to free climb the outside of the coed dorm I lived in. The three floors above me were all female and I would go window to window and flirt with the girls as I climbed.

Another one of the tricks my friends and I used to pull to impress girls was probably about the dumbest. A friend of mine would be driving my car at highway speed and then I would roll down the passenger window and climb out onto the roof, then slide across, climb in the driver's side window and take over driving. We drove fast and took chances and everything we did was about taking it as far as we could go.

As an adult, I hear about kids dying doing stupid stuff like this all the time. A lot of times I think it would be nice to be bullet proof still, but most of the time I spend contemplating the fact that I never was.

Early in 1993, I beat the snot out of my next door neighbor in our dorm. We hated each other. In my defense (and opinion), the guy was a jerk. Still, he didn't deserve the beating I gave him. He went to the hospital and I went to jail. I was charged with a couple of felonies, and thanks to my grandparents paying for an attorney and a merciful judge, I was convicted of misdemeanor assault.

I had gotten into a lot of trouble before that, mostly for traffic or underage alcohol-related offenses, and was on probation. After the fight, my probation was revoked, and I ended up serving forty-five days of a ninety day jail sentence. Thirty days was for seriously damaging another person, and sixty days was for bouncing a thirteen dollar check. I am still trying to figure out the math on that one.

The small county jail I was in held several people that were on their way to prison. There were only about fifteen inmates at any given time, so we all got to know each other pretty well. Through witnessing their lives being ripped apart, and seeing what going to prison was doing to them and their families, it became clear to me how my family must be suffering as a result of my actions. Watching my mother and grandmother cry as the judge passed my sentence was one of the worst feelings I can ever remember.

Two things happened for me during this time of my life. First, and I know what you are going to say—yes, I found God. Not in the way I expected though.

Second, I decided that I did not want to spend another second in jail. This unfortunately would not be the case, but this realization drastically shaped my decision making skills and, consequently, my life.

Right after I got out of jail, another life shaping event happened. As may or may not be expected, I had developed and nurtured some pretty healthy rage issues through my youth. I still liked to fight and I really didn't know any other way to express anger or disagreement. Things were as simple as black and white to me. If you disagree with me, we fight about it. You are wrong, and I am right. I win, you lose. Done deal.

Well, one of these black and white moments unfolded at a hotel during a family reunion in South Dakota and I got in a fight with my cousin. We'd been sneaking some alcohol from the parents and things got a little out of hand.

When I do something, I am all in. Fighting is no different. I fight with rage and ferocity, and was putting on quite a show. Mid-scuffle, my mother marched over and snatched me by the arm and set me down hard in one of those vinyl-strap lounge chairs by the pool. It was then that she told me, very bluntly, that I was just like my father. I said I wasn't anything like my father. My Mom told me I didn't even know my father. I said I did.

Then, she laid it on me. "Ron isn't your dad," she said. "Your real dad was a biker named Greg and he was mean and nasty and you are just like him."

16

I found out all kinds of crazy things after that. Not the least crazy of which was that my mother, my only lifelong friend, was an ex-biker-bitch and my bio-dad was a gangster. Wow! Talk about a kick in the teeth! Needless to say, I was stunned and angry for being lied to.

I had a ton of questions after that. I interrogated everyone involved; my grandparents, my Mom, her friends from the time. Mom's story is so much more interesting than mine. Hopefully one day, you will read her book.

She had hidden her pregnancy from him because she was afraid; and, for good reason. I won't go into all of the gory details, but let's just say that our survival was in question. Once she knew for sure she was pregnant with me, my grandparents hid her from him in the small town in Southwest Kansas where I was born; and, as far as I know, he still doesn't know I exist.

Anyway, she hid me from bio-dad and him from me, partly because she was afraid that I would turn out like him. Genetics or not, I found a way to do that on my own and it scared her. As angry as I was with her at that time, I am glad she told me. Knowing about Greg, the fear of ending up in prison and the shame I felt for continuing to hurt those I loved really helped me turn things around in my life.

Soon after getting out of jail, I met my first wife. Then, in 1994, at the age of twenty-one, my first child was born. With Kyle's arrival three things happened. First (and immediately), I realized what true love really was. Second, I realized I needed to get my shit together in a big damn hurry. And, third, all of my priorities got turned on their head. I began wishing I had done better at NWMSU and had taken my life a little more seriously than I had.

I became ravenously ambitious and terrified of failure. My first wife and I moved to St. Louis so I could attend Broadcast Center in Clayton.

While attending school, I worked as a warehouse worker for a picture frame supply company in Earth City. After all, I needed a "real job", right? As was common throughout my early adult life, I also worked thirty hours a week as a dishwasher and cook at a popular wing and breast joint, and about fifteen hours a week as a door man at a local nightclub on the East Side.

In addition to the three jobs, I also went to school majoring in Business Administration at St. Louis Community College. This time around I did pretty well. I carried a 3.8 GPA, tutored math between classes, became a member of Phi Theta Kappa, volunteered as "The Reading Rabbit" at a daycare, and was invited to the National Dean's List.

My little girl was born in 1996 and she was a picture of mischievous perfection!

My motivation doubled.

Between two kids, school and three jobs, I never slept. I was exhausted. That same year I had a severe anxiety attack on the interstate while driving the family to work and daycare, and almost killed all of us. Naturally, I decided to take a few days off from everything. Consequently, I was fired from the nightclub. I was not devastated.

Eventually, I was offered a promotion at my "real job" so I dropped college and the wing joint job and moved to Atlanta, Georgia in 1998. It is worth noting that if I had stayed at the wing joint as a line cook and dedicated all of my time to them, I would have made a few thousand more dollars per year than my "real job" offered me to move to Atlanta; and, my career in the restaurant business would likely be much farther along. But, I'd be in a different place. Life is about choices. As bad as things went after that, I don't think I would change much.

In Atlanta, I worked as a purchasing agent earning *almost* twenty four thousand dollars a year. I hated it. To supplement my income from my "real job", guess what I did. Yep, I waited tables.

Eventually, this move to Atlanta resulted in three things, divorce, a deep dive into depression and a bottle of rum, and termination from the company I had dedicated my life to for six years. I was devastated.

Poor me. I got dumped for being an asshole and fired from a job I hated at a company I loved for being a drunk. I wallowed in self pity for a long time. It was years before I could accept the fact that these things "happening to me" were entirely my fault.

Later that year, I entered a restaurant in Cartersville, Georgia to apply for a serving job. I needed some kind of income while I searched for a "real job". As always, when looking for a job, I had on a suit and tie and had my résumé in hand. As luck would have it, the General Manager was the one to greet me. I handed him my résumé and let him know I would make a great server in his establishment.

Without saying a word he quickly scanned my résumé, and then he looked up at me in my suit and tie, and back at my résumé. He then pulled a business card from his shirt pocket, scrawled a name and phone number on the back of it and said, "No you won't. Call this girl and tell her you want to interview for the Assistant Manager position for me. I will let her know to expect your call. Call me if you have any questions."

Stunned and excited, I rushed home. I called the number on the back of the card and the woman answered. I said what the

GM had asked me to say, and scheduled the interview for the next day.

The day after that, they offered me the position.

The day after that, I began my career.

I had just landed my first real job.

THE TRANSFORMATION

Several years later, as a result of my actions and decisions, I would eventually have an all out mental break down and an experience that would change me deeply and forever.

After my first divorce, I met a girl from Georgia. Soon after the divorce was final, she and I were married. We really had a lot of fun together, traveling the world and partying and doing a lot of things that young couples do.

In spite of the few good things about us, my relationship with her embodies many of the worst parts of my life. We hated each other. Passionately. We spent five hellish years together and finally—and mercifully—divorced in 2005.

Once again, I coped with this "loss" by drinking too much and taking everything I did to the utmost extremes. I wasn't so much sad, as I was celebrating my freedom. I just celebrated all the time and way too hard!

In the summer of 2005, I received a DUI, I quit my desk job, and my house was repossessed by the bank. Failure had purposefully sought me out, once again, and set upon me with crushing results.

One night in November, I was out with my friends at our favorite bar. I began looking around the room. Everyone was so happy and, even though I was laughing and smiling, I was not. They all looked so truly happy and I was just exhausted from faking it. I was miserable.

My mind began spinning and all of the horrible things that had happened to me in my life were just parading through my head. I began to get very, very sad. I remember that one thought going through my head over and over—*I can't take it anymore.*

I was seriously contemplating suicide. The plan: I would just walk the five and a half miles home and end it. Pills would have to do. I didn't have a gun and I was too much of a pansy to even think about cutting any part of myself. If I still wanted to kill myself when I got home, I would do it. Decision made, I quietly paid my tab, and left the bar.

The walk home was *exactly* five and a half miles from door to door, and I could walk it in just over an hour. Having no driver's license, I had made the walk or bike ride many times. Shortly after beginning, a cold, steady rain started falling. Perfect.

As lighting flashed and thunder rumbled over Des Moines, my mind was racing. I grew angrier and more frightened at the prospect of taking my own life. Finally, I realized that I didn't want to die; and, I didn't want to live like this anymore. Naturally, I assigned blame.

I blamed God.

I began to verbally argue with The Lord. I admit, it was a pretty one sided argument—for a while. Looking back, I still laugh at the vision of me walking along the road yelling at the sky, meanwhile God is chuckling above as one single dark raincloud follows only me—Charlie Brown style—drenching me to the bone with ice cold precipitation while the rest of Des Moines was bathed in unseasonably warm weather.

My mantra, self centered as always, "Either help me, or leave me alone! I can't take anymore. I have failed the test!" I shouted this over and over becoming more and more arrogant and vociferous as I marched, refusing to be daunted or humbled by this rain.

Suddenly, I felt a soft, warm explosion, and then quick, sharp pain in the back of my head. My vision was absorbed by warmth and light. I fell to my hands and knees as intense and very realistic visions of the faces of my kids, my grandparents, my

24

parents, and all of my wonderful friends burst to life in succession before my blinded eyes. I could hear laughter and feel joy. Sudden, vivid memories of all of the beautiful places and things I have ever seen flooded my mind and I felt all of the awe and power of nature, and the love of my family fill my heart and soul at once in that brief moment.

Tears of shame filled my eyes, I began to cry. The message was clear. "You arrogant bastard." God just gave me the holy finger.

Calming my pace—and attitude—the rest of the way home, I saw all of the gifts I had been blessed with as clear as day. Never have I ever felt more selfish, foolish, or ashamed. And then, it was gone. The pain and the sadness were gone. I also had a terrible feeling of emptiness. God had left me for now. My true test was about to begin.

That night I came to a clear conclusion. I wasn't going to live like this anymore. And, I wasn't going to chicken out by killing myself.

I was going to make better decisions. There was only one person in this vast world who could make my life better, and that was me. And I was going to do it! Nobody would stop me from improving my life. Nobody.

First, I decided that I would just let the abuse, the bullying, and the regret and sadness go. It had been long enough.

I literally just decided to accept it—and let it go. Nothing could change the fact that it happened; so, why spend a minute more on it?

Then, I decided to get a better paying job and not to settle for one I didn't love. And I did it. I decided to be a positive person and to compliment people for their attributes rather than to judge them and chastise them for their faults, and I did it. I chose to eliminate the few people from my life who were persistently negative influences and consistently made me feel badly in any way, and I did it.

This positive decision making became a thing. I made a game of it. I would change little things, or big things. Anytime I felt a negative impact on me from an internal or external source, I changed it. I accepted things I couldn't change and found work-arounds for them. I gave up fighting for my house and took the loss as I moved to a shitty apartment, that I could afford, close to work. I focused on developing more positive friendships. I helped people more. My life changed for the better immediately and dramatically.

First, I tripled my income inside of a year. I got my first GM job. I met my wife, who I have been with for almost ten years now (third time's a charm!). My career continues to advance and I continue to learn and develop as a leader and as a person. My third child was born. My fourth is on the way. I developed many long, unbreakable friendships.

My life is a long damn way from perfect. I am a long damn way from perfect. But I learned a valuable lesson that rainy night in November 2005. That lesson is that the life I lead is very much up to me.

Things are going to happen to us that we cannot predict or control, and once they happen, there is no going back. But, no matter how bad it was, the worst parts are over. It has happened. There is not a damn thing that you, me, God, or anyone else can do about it. What you can control however is how you *choose* to let it affect you and your future. You *can* control how you *choose* to represent your past.

If you choose to be angry at the world and everyone in it, then understand that it is a choice. *Your choice.* If you choose to wallow in doubt and self pity because of all the bad things that have happened to you, instead of charging forward, then remember that *you* chose that.

The good news is that it is never too late to change your choices. The power is yours. Trust me, it seems *much* harder right now than it really is. You have the power to change, and to change your life. All you have to do—is choose.

First, you must decide what you want your life to look like, then eliminate the roadblocks that are preventing you from achieving that vision. Once you make the decision, you must be absolutely committed to achieving it. Don't let anyone stand in your way live your life for you first, and others second. I'm not saying be a narcissistic pain in the rear, but take care of number one. You can't care for others as effectively if you aren't healthy first.

Sometimes that might mean ending long relationships or changing long held beliefs or completely reshaping how you view the world. Not easy stuff.

You deserve to be happy and successful, so make the choice now! Be happy! Be successful!

You will fail. You will falter. You will fall back on old ways and hard times. A clear path can become muddied from time to time. And, if you are committed to making the necessary positive changes in your life and accepting the past for what it is, then jumping over the mud puddles gets easier and easier the more you practice.

I hate to fail. But it's okay. I have a lot of failure ahead of me I'm sure. So do you. Let's agree that we will never let the fear of failure stop us from trying; and, we will never let the reality of failure stop us from trying again.

PART ONE

ATTITUDE

CHAPTER ONE

FIRST, LOVE IT

You may find this shocking, but I have written this book from a restaurant manager's perspective. It's okay though, it won't be a very hard stretch for you to apply this to your own field. The ideas in this book are easily transferrable to any segment of hospitality or customer service. If you deal with people for a living, I think you will find value in these pages.

My experience as a manager taught me a lot of things about business, but even more about people. Being a student of people is important in any industry and it is absolutely crucial in customer service. To me there are really six types of people in the hospitality business, and I think this could apply to any industry. For me, at least, these were almost stages in my career more than a "type".

1. The Greenhorn. You are new to the industry. You've never been here, and you don't truly know what to expect, but somebody somewhere (maybe you) thought you'd be good at it. You are my favorite person to hire. You are enthusiastic, you know that you don't know, and you don't know what you don't know—and that makes you easily moldable.

As a team member you may lack direction, or even be fearful or confused about your future. You may not know what you want to do with your life and you may just be working here because you need a job. Don't be afraid! This business is fantastic and a lot of fun, and you can also make a ton of money. Also, it has a stigma attached to it, by some, as a less-than-desirable career choice. Not true. I personally know servers and bartenders who make fifty-grand a year, and it isn't all that hard to do.

As a manager, brace yourself. You are in for a ride. If you have never managed a restaurant before, it will get worse before it gets better. A mentor of mine early in my career told me that if I could make it past six months, I'd be okay. Not the most encouraging advice I ever received, but it turned out to be true. Almost magically at the six month mark my confidence really took hold and I began making things happen. Most likely this won't be true for everyone, but it has been true for nearly every single new manager I have ever worked with over my long career.

As an owner that is new to the business, all of the previous comments apply, but also you can be dangerous and irresponsible. I recommend spending a year working under a good GM before you buy, or hiring someone you trust—an experienced owner or manager—as a consultant and then listen to them. Trust me, I have seen really smart people flush literally hundreds of thousands of dollars because they bought a place thinking that their experience in the XYZ business paired with the fact that they liked food and drink would make them a good bar or restaurant owner.

2. The Coaster. It's a job. Maybe it's a second job for you to supplement your income from your "real job". Maybe it's money to get beers after class. You are experienced and may only be here for a while, it's not your career, but merely a stepping stone—and that's okay. You are a tough nut to crack as you are probably just along for the ride and aren't super concerned about being a top contributor. You are happy to fly just under the radar and make your cash. And, that is just fine with me. In this business you are an important part of the team, just remember that it is easier to fly under the radar when you do the things you are supposed to do.

3. The Old Salt. Sorry Salty, you are my least favorite of the six. You are either consciously or subconsciously pissed off because you are however old and still managing, bartending, waiting tables, or cooking. You have seen it all before and no one can tell you anything new. You probably are praying for a way

out but you just don't know what else you could do at this point in your life. You are jaded from years of giving and giving, and your emotional return on investment has been low as you have begun buying your own negative bullshit. Dealing with the public has taken its toll on you, and you are probably exhausted and stressed a lot.

Your attitude and experience do more to hurt the business than to help it—in spite of the ten or fifteen regulars that you point to whenever I try give you feedback or coach you about your attitude. You probably spend a lot of time bitching to and about management and finding fault in the way everything is done—and you may be totally right! You either fail to see or care *how* to help fix it, though, and your bedpost is hacked up with the score marks of all the people you have turned to your side. Relax though, I have been there. The really good news is that with a little desire, a motivated and inspirational boss and a good coach, we can get you out of this rut and make things exciting again! But, you have to meet us half way. We have some choices to make in the coming pages, and I want to help you with this.

4. The Solid Contributor. You are a cousin to The Coaster. This may not be your first—or even third—choice of career, but something inside you prevents you from being able to fly under the radar. You are driven for excellence and thrive on being recognized for your contributions either privately or publicly. You are a stud manager, host, server, cook, or bartender.

You will probably leave me for a "real job" some day, but you are going to give me a hundred percent while you are here. And I love you for it...deeply.

5. The Disciple. You are married to this business. You are obsessed. Your passion for service and hospitality are unmatched in any circle. Maybe you got a taste at a young age, and you never looked back. Maybe you developed this sense of pride and loyalty over time and experience. Maybe it's because it's the family business, or you are just wired that way. Whatever the reason, you are committed and driven for excellence and you would be happy doing what we do for the rest of your life. You may take yourself a little too seriously, though, and anxiety leads to the Salty Dark Side, so relax a little and enjoy the ride.

6. The Vet. You have seen it all. Maybe you didn't see yourself ending up here after all these years but you have accepted it and you are content. You enjoy what you do and you are happy with your decision to commit. You may still look back at old pictures and wonder "what if I had tried just a little harder to get my band signed" but the grown up in you knows better. You recognize the power you have to positively impact people's lives and you love taking care of people. And you are damn good at it! You probably went through many or all of the first five stages, and you might again. Whatever your path, you are in this for life and you wouldn't have it any other way. This is me.

Look, the customer service and hospitality business—like any other business where you deal with people—is not easy and the emotional return can be low at times. The secret is simple and somehow incredibly difficult for people at the same time: *You have to love it first.*

If you don't love it, or can't find your way back to the fold, then just go. Trust me, do yourself a huge favor and call it quits. There are lots of things you can do for money and if you are miserable doing what you do, then you need to get out for your own health and sanity—and for that of your family. Maybe you just need a break so you can get your head right, but if you don't love taking care of people and creating joy for people through food, drink and hospitality then you are in for a really long and stressful journey, and you are going to take a lot of good people with you. You have to be able to connect to the magic that happens each and every day, and you have to be able to create it. It is all but impossible to be successful in this business of customer service and hospitality if you are bitter that you are here.

Think of it like this: There is no neutral energy. You are either giving energy, or taking it away. This point cannot be stressed enough! It is just not possible for you to be neutral. Try this; the next time you are out with friends try to take what you feel is an attitude-neutral/energy-neutral stance in the group. Depending on whether you are normally more positive or more negative, a giver or a taker, I guarantee that someone will ask you what the hell is wrong with you, or why you are in such a good mood inside of five minutes. You are either giving to, or taking from that person, and the others, because you have changed the dynamic of the group. Now, everyone is focused on you. You have effectively given, or depleted energy. Be the one giving.

I don't care if you are the guy flipping burgers or the president and CEO of the next big thing—Love it. Love makes this business great. Whatever industry has chosen you, whatever job you have, whatever role you fill, find the greatest things about your position and enjoy yourself. If you can do that, you will always be successful. That is the spirit and foundation of true hospitality. It can really be argued that true hospitality is the foundation of great leadership. If you are a master of hospitality, then the rest is simply a matter of a ton of dedication, a bit of technical prowess, a basic understanding of math, drive and direction.

Now, all of that being said, love can get you in trouble. You don't have to love the company you work for, it fact, I recommend you don't. Your company can't love you back, no matter how great you are. Falling in love with a company can make you blind, and lead you to make poor decisions that would cause you and your family harm. You can be loyal, and you can be proud—and I do recommend working for a company that you feel loyal to and proud to work for, but I'd recommend stopping short of love. Keep yourself dispassionate about the company and passionate about your product and your people. I propose that The Emotional Chain of Command (ECC) should go like this:

1. You. First and most important, you must be happy doing what you are doing and who you do it for. If you are miserable, you cannot be an effective human (or leader) or live up to your full potential. So, as selfish as it may sound, love yourself first. You will always have to make sacrifices in life, just know where your line is and try not to cross it. If you find yourself on the wrong side of that line, find your way back as fast as you can.

2. Your Family. Once you have affixed your own mask, focus on your loved ones. Make certain that your work does not negatively impact those you love the most. This will go a long way toward your own happiness and success.

3. Your Team. You are happy, your family is happy. Now focus all of your energy learning about the people you work with and developing relationships with them to their full potential. Make work about them, not you. Teach them, learn from them. Since you are happy and able to realize your own full potential, they will benefit from your experience and joy in life, and you will benefit from theirs.

4. Your Product. Be passionate and proud about what you do! Love your product and defend its quality passionately and without fail!

5. Your Customers or Guests. Yep, they are Fifth. Sounds counter-intuitive but it all goes back to the oxygen mask analogy. If you are fulfilled and happy, your family is fulfilled and happy and your team is fulfilled and happy, and you are all passionate about the product you sell, then your guests cannot lose!

6. Your Boss. It's okay to love your boss and anyone else in the chain of command. Please remember, it is their duty to defend the company and the decisions they make will reflect that duty. It is in everyone's best interest that they treat you with the same love and respect as you treat your team and colleagues. When they make decisions that you disagree with, you have to be able to control the way you feel about that. It is very difficult sometimes.

As with true love, professional love is based on trust, respect and admiration. Those are three very fragile components, and if one or more of them is perceived as broken on either side, it can be easy to feel hurt and betrayed. Go into it with a clear head and a clear understanding of the reality of their primary responsibility to the company, just as they should understand that your primary responsibility is to your family and yourself. You have to have a good relationship with your boss. This should ideally be a two way street and your boss should be able to count on you, and you should feel heard and respected.

7. Your Company. Remember, a company is a sign. It's a product. It's a balance sheet. It is brick and mortar. But most importantly, it is a group of people with a common mission—to provide great service, hospitality and product to other people. If all of the people in that equation are fulfilled and happy, then the company's mission will ultimately be achieved. Love your product. Love the people. Work for them, develop them, serve them with all of your heart and defend them vigorously.

Take a second to think about the way you behave at work. Honestly look back at your week, and try to hear yourself speaking to other people. Are you complaining about a decision, a boss, a guest, or a coworker? We have all done it. I want you to think about how one complaint when spoken to another person can influence the entire work place. Discontent spreads like fire in dry brush. As a boss, I can tell you a couple of things about this. One, is that if you have a valid complaint and you bring it to me in a constructive way, I am happy to listen to you. It may not be something I can change right away, or at all, but we can talk about it.

Second, if you are a chronic complainer and a person who just won't stop spreading dissent, we as managers have a name for you. You are called cancer. We don't care how good you are at the technical parts of your job, we don't care how long you have been with the company. After coaching, counseling and discussion, if you choose to perpetuate this behavior, we will cut the cancer out so that the rest of the body may live.

Complaining and negativity are destructive to you, destructive to everyone around you, and we cannot allow it. If you are this person, and you will not respond positively to coaching, trust me when I say that you will eventually be fired for it. You are likely anxious when new managers start at your company because you have your current management team held hostage, and you are afraid the newbie will see past your crap and ask you to change. Change is scary for most people, and it is a necessary component of a successful business.

Remember, being right is only half the battle. Negativity and spreading dissent completely negate your correctness in any and every instance. You must learn how to bring your frustrations to light in positive ways and use your knowledge and experience to help others around you grow and improve.

If you are the chronic complainer, consider this: What is more important to you, being right, or changing the situation you are complaining about? There are ways to change the situation, and none of them involve complaining and displaying a negative attitude.

So, love what you do! Love taking care of people and brightening other's days. Love yourself, your family, your team, your boss, and your guests. Respect your company, and be passionate about the product you serve. And have fun! If you can't do it, it's fine but <u>you</u> will be miserable and the other parts of the ECC will suffer. Your Emotional ROI will be next to zero, and life is too short. Find something you love to do, and do it. And, when you do have a complaint or you aren't feeling good about things at work, find someone above you and find a productive way to talk about things.

My loving and wonderful Grandmother Mary always told me, "Tony, I don't care if you grow up to be a ditch digger. Be the best darn ditch digger out there." And I have always tried. No matter what ditch I happen to be digging, I always want to be the best at it. I love you Grandma, thank you for the great advice.

CHAPTER TWO

UNDERSTAND THE PASSION

How many times have you dealt with an upset guest? If you have been in business for any length of time, probably more than a couple. So, now let me ask you how many times you or one of your colleagues say something snide or sarcastic about the guest to explain or downplay the reason they might be upset? Have you ever gotten upset with a server, front desk clerk at a hotel, or on the phone with a customer service representative? Take a minute to think about *why* you did.

I will tell you, I don't think a lot of people truly know off of the top of their heads. People mask it with words and phrases like "the customer is always right" and "customer service". You know you deserve to be treated respectfully, and you know you expect a certain level of excellence when you spend your hard earned money on something, but do you really know why?

42

That is a lot of questions, so let me cut through the clutter and give you my theory. I preach this concept to my team as if it is scientific fact, although I have never done any more scientific research than just pay attention.

To set this up, we need to go on a quick journey. You have to play along for this point to come through.

I want you to come with me to your favorite restaurant—a nice, sit down place with great food and great atmosphere. The music and lighting are perfect and the smell of amazing food permeates every square inch of the place. You work here. You could be the manager, a server, cook, host—it really doesn't matter, other than the fact that you have a very important role in the outcome of this story.

I want you to pick your role and imagine yourself in full uniform, standing in the bustling dining room full of people. Close your eyes for a moment and imagine yourself standing there. Every table is seated and people are eating, drinking wine, and talking.

Look around and try to imagine what people are wearing, what they are eating and what they are talking about.

Now, imagine everyone is visiting with one another except for an elderly couple sitting toward the back in a booth. They are methodically picking through their food in silence. They don't seem particularly upset, but more disinterested. You've seen them before a few times and know them to be good regulars, John and Sally. You approach them and begin a conversation. That's when you find out that John has just been diagnosed with cancer at the hospital across the street. After learning the diagnosis, they wanted to come eat here because it is their favorite place to be, and they just want to feel better about this short, fragile life for a minute. You walk away and you hear them continue talking about their first date fifty years ago.

As you look around at the wonderful assortment of people eating here tonight, notice the couple on their first date. There is the high power executive treating some potential clients to some steaks and a few beers—they are about to spend millions with his company, and the commission will pay for his oldest son's college tuition.

The couple engaged in a quiet but intense argument. The parents meeting their son's girlfriend for the first time. Oh! What's this? A young man has just dropped to his knee and offered a modest but gleaming diamond to his beautiful bride to be, and she said yes! The dining room erupts in applause. Two tables over, a man fights back tears and signs the divorce papers his wife brought to this last meal they may ever share together. In the table right next to theirs, a young woman gives her new husband a card unexpectedly, the word 'Congratulations' neatly scribed on the front. He is perplexed, and she is absolutely beaming. Tears fill his eyes and joy fills his soul as he opens the

44

card to find the very first picture, a sonogram, he's ever seen of his first child.

Magic happens at our tables and in your business each and every day. This principle and the rest of those I will share in this book are applicable to any job in any industry. I have been blessed enough to see all of these things and many more in my career. The point is this: Sharing food and drink with others is far more important than simply eating or drinking. It is intimate. It is intense. We don't really think about the intensity because really, by age forty, you have eaten some forty five thousand meals and hundreds of thousands of snacks. It's automatic. We just do it. We don't *think* about the love and the intimacy and passion—the carnal intensity—that goes into it, but it is there.

The fact is that people can sustain themselves at home. You can get life giving calories from all kinds of terrible things. If you have the privilege of serving people, then those people came to you for something much more special than sustenance; even though they themselves may not really be aware of it. It is the duty of every individual in your organization to protect the excellence of that experience. That is the spirit of hospitality that truly makes a business great.

Now, go back to the dining room scene. Close your eyes again and imagine the room, the lighting, the smell of the food and all of the people we talked about. Imagine the love, the passion, the sadness and joy and pain.

The intensity.

What was your favorite story?

Who can you imagine most clearly?

Think about them for a moment. Think about *why* they chose to spend their time with *you* here tonight. Do you have your favorite picked out?

What are they wearing?

What are they eating?

Can you imagine how they are feeling?

How sad, or happy, or frightened they might be?

Now, I want you to imagine that *you* ruined their meal.

CHAPTER THREE

THE HARD TRUTH

There is a growing trend of entitlement that I and contemporaries of mine in all lines of business are recognizing in the hiring pool. Businesses are bending to it. Books are being written about it. There is a lot of blame put on generational gaps and idiosyncrasies, and that's fine. There is enough science and psychology behind generational theory to pay it due attention, and if you don't strive to understand it, you will certainly fall behind. But I think there is a bigger fundamental problem.

Personally, I don't think this "entitlement complex", this complete disregard for what I will refer to as traditional work ethic, is so easily explained by generational differences—and, to me, it's a crappy excuse even if it was. I have had fifty year old men look me dead in the face and tell me that something I asked them to do was not their job, and expect to make $15.00/hr just because they show up for work sometimes.

A lot of kids I hire today don't even know how to use a broom properly. We recently terminated a young man for threatening our Executive Chef, and the kid was just stunned. Many people in the lower echelons of the work force seem to feel that they get a prize just for showing up. Recently, I was doing some research on a site called Glassdoor.com and reading reviews about what people think of their jobs—across many categories of business. People were saying things like "I have to work too hard" and "They expect too much" and "the standards are too high". They list these things as cons! These aren't cons! These things are great! Bring me more work, bring me high standards, bring me a boss that expects a lot from me so that I have to work hard to impress him or her. Even if I fail I am higher than I would have otherwise been! It is shocking to me that people really think this way. This is a mentality that I will never understand or tolerate in my business.

Maybe you do. If so, let's work on that a bit. And, if you believe that effort is enough, or if you were raised in a "ribbon for participation" environment, this is an important chapter for you. Here it is.

The Hard Truth: The world owes you exactly nothing. Results matter more than effort and participation. Trying really hard and failing is still failing. If you want something, then work really hard for it because nobody that cares about you is just going to hand it to you. You do not get a ribbon or points just for participation. If you find this unfair, tough. That's the way it is. Second place is the first loser. The quicker you accept and understand this, the quicker you will move ahead. And to this end, there is no substitute for a solid work ethic, internal drive and having the gumption to look fear and failure dead in the eye and back them down. Successful people fail—a lot. Successful people arguably fail more so than unsuccessful people, because they have the backbone to stand up straight, dust themselves off, and try again.

This isn't to say that you are going to succeed on the backs of others. This has nothing to do with being unethical. In fact, this may be the most fair and ethical principle in business, capitalism, and nature. The strongest and best survive, so work hard to find and prove your value. Mediocrity was never intended by our creator—whether you believe that to be God, ancient astronauts, or pure evolution—to survive.

CHAPTER FOUR

UNDERSTAND YOURSELF

"God, grant me Serenity to accept the things I cannot change; Courage to change the things I can; And Wisdom to know the difference."—*Serenity Prayer*

Sometimes—many times—our biggest roadblocks come from within. As humans we can tend to over think issues and get wrapped up in the minutia of seemingly overwhelming challenges when the simplest solution is staring us right in the face. How many times have you been faced with a new task that was so intimidating, but when you got through it you were shocked at how simple it really was? The choice of the word simple—over the word easy—is intentional. The Serenity Prayer is often used in addiction recovery programs. If challenging yourself and making needed changes was easy, well then we would not have therapists, twelve-step programs, and chances are you wouldn't have paid for this book. I contend it is easier than most people think, however. The first step can feel impossible, but each subsequent step gets easier.

As with addiction programs, the road to self-development begins with recognizing and accepting that you have a need, or a problem. This, for me was the most difficult part. How do you admit that you are flawed, or imperfect? It's easy to say, "nobody is perfect" to make yourself or someone else feel better when a mistake is made. It is much harder to look at yourself in the mirror and recognize and admit that a fundamental set of behaviors and thoughts needs to be challenged and changed. It is harder still to take your first step down that path.

Think about it like this; parents commonly say things to their kids like "be yourself" and "be proud of who you are". All good advice, except for a couple of problems. Problem One: This is the narrative that kids play through their minds far into adulthood. "I'm not changing because I am proud of who I am!" or "that's just who I am, deal with it!" I have heard these things spoken out loud more times that I care to remember, sometimes by myself. We are effectively laying a big roadblock out for our kids by giving them these kinds of blanket platitudes.

There are all kinds of ways we can teach kids self-confidence, *and* self-reflection. Problem Two: Most parents are relatively young when their first kids are born. In many cases, their parents were relatively young when they were born, and generationally on and on all the way down trunk of the family tree.

The way I am raising my six year old is _vastly_ different than the way I raised my eighteen and twenty year olds. I am better tempered, wiser, smarter, more patient, more reflective, more experienced and all around much more well equipped to be a good parent who teaches the importance of accountability, confidence, financial responsibility, humility, and accurate self-reflection. Especially if you are a first child, then you are paying for your parent's inexperience in some ways. It's compounded if you are the first child of a first child, and so on.

One trait I deal with rather frequently in people I work with is an almost intentional self-obstruction. It is a near refusal to find, recognize and accept the easiest course of action, thereby making the process of change excruciating for all of those involved. There is also a very frightening lack of people brave enough, or willing enough, to take the time to honestly investigate the possibility that many of the problems they face might just be self-inflicted. Also, it can be difficult, when you are a person who looks at yourself first in the face of adversity, to know when to stop looking inward and begin to focus your energies on external factors; and, even harder still to effectively handle those factors.

Change the things you can, internal or external, and learn to work with or around the things you can't. With time and experience, success and failure, you will become skilled and wise enough to know the difference.

Not many people get promoted by staying in their comfort zone, or refusing to accurately self-evaluate, so what we are really talking about is change, right? People hate change! They resist it. They make it harder than it has to be. I have seen people claw and fight tooth and nail to keep things at the status quo, even when the status quo is terrible, and the change would benefit them greatly. Comfort should be a four letter word for you, at least in business. Comfort breeds complacency. Complacency breeds mediocrity. Mediocrity is a cancer that breeds failure, and it must be exterminated.

In order to have productive change, you need to understand yourself. Understand your own quirks, shortcomings and flaws. Learn to recognize the roadblocks that you set up for yourself. It involves taking a real good hard look in the mirror, and sometimes you won't like what you see, but that is fine. That means you have found a good starting point. Don't get overwhelmed. Take things one step at a time.

There is an old Bill Murray movie called What About Bob? where Bob (Bill Murray) is a neurotic man stricken with multiple phobias who ends up basically stalking a self-help author Dr. Leo Marvin (Richard Dreyfus) who wrote about baby steps being the key to true self-improvement. While the movie is hysterical, the fictional book's premise holds up. Small steps add up to significant improvement over time.

People are generally pretty easy to fool. As social beings we learn to trust one another and take people at face value. You can successfully lie to anyone you want, at least for a while; but, you cannot lie to yourself. No matter how hard you try, when you are alone at night in the dark staring up at the ceiling, or staring yourself in the face as you brush your teeth, only you know the truth about yourself. And, only you can initiate the *real* changes in your own life that you need to make to be successful.

Once you really understand and realize how much power you have and how in control of your own destiny you really are, you will be able to successfully challenge yourself, challenge your fears, and change. From the voice of experience my friend, let me tell you, hold on tight because your life will change in a big damn hurry. From the time that I made this determination for myself to the time I landed my first GM position was about 2 years.

CHAPTER FIVE

PRACTICE WHAT YOU PREACH

This really should go without saying. But it doesn't.

You are going to have a very difficult time holding people to standards that you can't keep yourself. So, practice what you preach.

I worked for a guy one time, a GM of a Mexican food joint in Des Moines, who looked me right in the face and said, "I'll be honest with you, I am not going to do line checks, but as KM, I expect you to do it every shift."

Really? Okay. I did it of course because that is my work ethic and line checks are important. I spent a lot of time going through the line check book and filling out line checks that he had not done—as he had promised. I didn't mind, but I also didn't respect him.

Once, I rolled out a ten point cleaning checklist for my managers to use when they closed. This was born out of frustration over a constant neglect of seemingly obvious things to me and after many requests to my management team. I was frustrated at myself for not being able to figure out how to motivate them. I rolled this out to my management team poorly. It was rolled out to the hourly team even worse.

Immediately, people were angry. We introduced what to them seemed to them like a major change, even though my ten points were far less than the company mandated checklists required. I acted out of frustration, and it was implemented against the will of everyone but me. On the first day, the manager responsible for rolling out was at the restaurant until four a.m. the following morning! People were going to quit, I mean we are talking mutiny.

I had to look at myself and recognize that I had problems beyond my inability to motivate my management team. I had a management team I did not respect, who didn't respect me, and who were unmotivated and incapable of, or unwilling to recognize and correct the issues at hand. I had an hourly team who did not believe in the possibility that my standards could be met effectively. They felt that they would be at work far too late and most of them work day jobs. Also, I had a problem with my ability to hold people accountable effectively.

I looked deep and hard at the problem and myself, and I made five determinations. One, the ROI from the energy invested in my management team over the last year was nearly nonexistent and because of this lack of impact I was frustrated and angry toward them.

Two, I felt I could not change the managers through termination or otherwise so I decided to accept it for what it was.

Three, I determined that the standards were not unreasonable, impossible, or even difficult for that matter.

Four, I determined this was something that needed to change because it was causing me a great deal of distress.

And five, I determined I needed to work on my ability to hold people accountable more effectively.

I therefore decided that I could have the most impact with my hourly team by helping them remove some road blocks. So, I closed the restaurant one night with the guys and focused on teaching them not only *what* I was looking for but the *how* and *why*. My restaurant has never been cleaner. Everyone was off the clock by ten forty-five. And we all had a great time cleaning together. This took very little extra time on my part and I never had another problem getting my kitchen closed the way I wanted it. I then began studying the art of accountability more closely, and putting what I learned into practice.

As a person either in, or aspiring to be in, a leadership position please understand that leadership by example is crucial. If you are holding your team to a standard that you cannot, or will not, meet yourself, then there are one of two things that need to change in that equation*.

*Hint—it's not the people around you.

CHAPTER SIX

PROFESSIONALISM AND ETTIQUETTE

There are a lot of things that go into professionalism, and etiquette is a pretty fluid concept. I'm going to do my best to sum up what these things mean to me. It's like the famous quote by Justice Potter Stewart in 1964. Although, he was referring to pornography. Paraphrased:

"I can't define it, but I know it when I see it."

To me, professionalism is more noticeable when unprofessional behavior is absent. In other words, striving to act professional can come off as insincere or fake. Instead, really try to avoid being unprofessional. Doing or saying things that don't belong in the work place can mark you for life, so to speak. An inappropriate statement or unwelcome touch can get you fired, or even sued these days.

True professionals are students of their craft. I suggest that you strive for improvement each day. Look for ways to elevate your knowledge and standards. Learn the lingo, learn the science, delve into the art of self-improvement and an organic sense of professionalism will soon begin to crystallize. Frankly, it's going to be different in different places, and at different stages of the game. Perfection is an unattainable goal, but it is still the goal. If you are always reaching for the horizon, you may not reach it, but you will see the world!

I once worked for a company where Team Members are encouraged to refer to the Guests as ladies and gentlemen. In fact, one of our mantras was, "We are Ladies and Gentlemen Serving Ladies and Gentlemen". I was really struggling to develop this habit in my Team. So guess what? I decided that to inspire this habit in my team, I needed to elevate my own standards of communication. When speaking to my Team, I began addressing *them* as ladies and gentlemen. And you know, that habit was translated to our Guests almost immediately! Pretty cool!

Conversely, I think etiquette is more noticeable when it is present. You have to learn etiquette—work at it. The rules for golf, for example, or greeting dignitaries from other countries. Do unto others, as you would have done unto you. The heart of etiquette is respect. Going out of your way to do something kind for someone or doing a little something extra to show that you respect someone is very powerful relationship building behavior.

Mondays are usually a big day for me. Not to be cliché, but they are typically a very intense, grueling marathon day filled with counting, reporting, book keeping, forecasting, goal setting and tracking. I am at work by five in the morning, and best case I am out by four in the afternoon, but typically even later than that.

Once, on a particular Monday, I had a catering event for the coaches of the Indianapolis Colts. As usual, I was at work at five a.m. and I wrapped up at the restaurant around two thirty and we headed for the Farm Bureau Sports Complex. We finished up there around eight o'clock and got back to the restaurant around eight thirty.

Upon entering the restaurant's back door it was pretty clear that they had endured a pretty rough night. A couple of people had called off, and we had been much busier than expected. The place was a disaster! After a fifteen and a half hour work day it would have been pretty easy for me to toss up the deuces and get in my car and go home to leave my frazzled team to clean up the mess, but that is not how I do things. I strapped on an apron and spent the next two hours doing dishes and running trash to help them get caught up.

It makes people feel good to see you work to help them, and they know what you are sacrificing. They respect it. And the respect you earn is worth a thousand times any sacrifice that you make, I promise you that.

Now there will be certain etiquette behaviors your leader and your team may expect from you. There are certain behaviors in many situations that are nearly mandatory. As you navigate your way up the professional ladder, you will need to learn and respect those traditions. For example, you might check with everyone before they leave and ask if there is anything else you can do to be of service to the team.

You can introduce and create habits that you expect from those around you, at any level. Develop your own standards. If you make something important to you, those you work with will make it important to them. It's that simple. If they don't, then either you haven't found the right way to motivate them, or you hired poorly.

That brings me to professional buy in. Organizations around the globe have mission statements and values that they expect people to uphold and live by. These things can sometimes be awkward and uncomfortable at first, as is any new habit. However, they are critically important to the success of the unit and ultimately the company.

If your professional goal is to improve your situation, you must increase your value to the organization. To do that, you must buy in to these ideas. And, if you can demonstrate an ability to be a warrior for that culture, you drastically increase your value to the organization. The biggest raises and promotions are given to the most valuable people. Memorize the mission statement and core values of your company. Get comfortable integrating the system into your language and actions. Make every decision based in those ideas and concepts. Set the bar high for those around you, and hold them to it! If you can do that effectively, you are winning a big part of the battle already!

Buy in goes much further than simply flying the company colors. It also means that from time to time, you are going to have to support and enforce, to your highest ability, decisions that you may not personally agree with as passionately as you would if you had come up with the idea yourself. That can be really hard. But it is important. Don't take that to mean that you should do unethical or illegal things because your boss told you to. Or, that you should participate in activities that could damage the reputation of your business. You should never practice any of those behaviors! But, you and your boss will not see eye to eye on everything, and sometimes you are going to get vetoed. It shows your professional prowess to get behind the idea and support it as if you came up with it yourself.

Finally, represent your organization well. You speak not only for yourself in the way you choose to speak and behave in the public eye, but you speak for your organization as well. You have to understand that the people you choose to associate with and they ways in which you choose to interact with the world have an impact on your future. Surround yourself with successful people and you will greatly increase your chances of success. Understand when you make that nasty or negative comment on social media the impact that it has on people's perception of you and how that can impact your success in achieving your goals, and ultimately the success of your organization. Keep your dirty laundry where it belongs.

One of the best things that you can do if you are struggling to find a group of successful people to surround yourself with is find someone you respect and ask them to mentor you. This could be a boss, or a colleague. Typically this is someone who you view as successful in your industry. For example, I am actively mentoring three individuals who want my job. It is a valuable relationship, and not one to be entered into lightly. It's a commitment, and there are pretty intense obligations on both sides of the fence. You do not want to be perceived as someone who wastes another professional's most valuable resource—their time.

CHAPTER SEVEN

CHANGE YOUR PREPOSITION

As we discuss increasing your value to your organization. All we need to do is change one simple word into another. We need to change the word "to" to the word "for".

Stop allowing things to happen <u>to</u> you, and start making things happen <u>for</u> you. Somebody once said that luck is where hard work and opportunity meet. I contend that there are two other streets in this intersection. Positive attitude and good, well-informed decision making. It's never as difficult or as complicated as we make it seem in our own heads. Put these things in practice and take a step outside of yourself for a minute and look at your situation with an honest and critical eye, and the solution to your challenge is often pretty simple. I will never say easy. Changing course in your life and making radical life decisions that will change your paradigm is never easy, but it can have tremendous positive impact on the person you become and the way in which the world perceives you.

It's a matter of having goals, paying attention, and simply making better decisions that put you closer to achieving your goals.

I *love* the show "Bar Rescue". I may have seen every episode. Tonight, I was watching an episode where at the beginning John Taffer was doing his recon and watching a failing bar empty out on a Saturday Night under the crushing weight of terrible music from a terrible band. As it turns out, the bass player for the band was one of the owners of the bar. When Taffer challenged the man about this, he became very defensive and said he wasn't going to sit there and let somebody talk bad about his band! Does this sound like a business man who has his priorities straight? Does he have the right goals? Was he paying attention?

This guy may be out there making things happen for his band, but in the process he and his partner lost their life savings and their business. According to a story posted on Cincinatti.com, the owners placed a notice on their Facebook page blaming two unnamed individuals for undermining their efforts and taking the bar out from underneath them. I am not involved in the situation. Who knows what happened. To me it sounds like a couple of guys who got in over their heads and let their business fail through a combination of professional ignorance or arrogance, lack of common goals and vision, and delayed action.

Many years ago, I worked for a small local bar in Des Moines. The owner was very successful and the bar enjoyed a longstanding reputation of being the place in town where good people could go to have a good time. I began there as a door guy, and quickly worked my way up to management. The first year I was manager there, our bar did just shy of one million dollars in sales. Pretty huge for a little corner bar without a food menu! The owner had an executive background in human resources and really knew how to get the most from people. He rarely stepped foot in the place. The first three years I worked there were pretty awesome. We all made great money, we all had a great time, and we worked for a great man.

Soon after I became a manager, rumors began floating around that the bar had been sold. It wasn't long before we all learned the dreaded truth. The owner had sold our bar. Rumors always fly faster than truth, and there is a glimmer of truth in all rumors. I will tell you that the rumors were not good. Stories of the new owner and his girlfriend being unknowledgeable and unqualified were the mildest.

According to the rumor mill, the sale had been motivated by a need to raise funds for a new bar. I do not know for certain, but it is on pretty good authority that the bar sold for over five hundred thousand dollars. The new bar opened, the sale closed and the owner had asked me and my friend Cory to come with him to the new bar. Cory declined. I accepted.

This, for me, was a valuable lesson in doing what you love. I absolutely hated the new bar, but I refused to give up. The non-regular crowd was rude, the music was terrible, my ideas—which were highly valued at the old bar—were virtually ignored at the new bar. I was miserable, and it showed. My level of service and hospitality suffered. Soon I was being sucked into a vortex of my own misery. I complained a lot. Eventually the owner recognized that we were no longer a good fit for one another and made the decision to let me go, which I was thankful for.

Immediately, I was asked to bartend at a new bar with a friend. The owners were pretty well connected, and this place became a new hotspot for a while. Keep in mind that Iowa ranks near the top of the list of bars per capita, and new bars spring up like Starbucks in Seattle. The guys who owned this bar were very well intentioned but there were five partners, I think this was mistake number one of many. They all had decent business acumen. A couple had a lot of money and experience in other industries. None of them had any bar or restaurant experience to speak of.

We had a lot of fun. I drank more Hennessy in three months than any ten people should drink *ever*. The owners knew how to throw a party for sure, but everyone who came there were partying at the owners expense and they and all their relatives, friends and employees drank them straight out of business.

When I was first hired, I recognized a lot of very bad signs. By this time I had accumulated a lot of knowledge and experience in the industry. I offered right away to help and asked if they would like me to manage for them. I interviewed with the largest financial contributor to the partnership. They ultimately refused my offer. One of the owners was the acting GM and he just did not have the experience to make it work. Not long after this, I noticed little things were starting to go wrong. You know, small things like we were not being paid, and we were running short on minor supplies like beer, liquor and glassware. The owners approached me this time, but it was too late, I declined.

At this time, I learned that the new owner of my old bar was looking for another manager. I immediately went to meet with him and he hired me back. The following week, the other place locked the doors. The next couple of years would be some of the most successful and most maddening years of my professional career.

My friend Cory was the general manager at this time. He had been beaten down by a year and a half of dealing with the new owners. You hear rumors and second hand information, but for some reason we humans never feel satisfied until we learn for ourselves. A few months after I started, Cory left to get a job with a local distributor and he recommended to the new owners that I take his position. They offered me the GM position and I accepted.

69

The situation at the bar was bad. When I left, we were running pretty good numbers. We averaged close to twenty thousand dollars in sales per week bringing well over twenty percent to the bottom line. By the time I came back, sales were less than half what they were before and the spirit of the place was miserable, and the place was disgusting. The first thing we did was meet as a team and we cleaned the place top to bottom, and we talked about some ideas to build sales—and we did. Thanks to a great team of people, who are all close friends of mine to this day, we had a pretty exciting and successful year for top line sales, tips and fun.

At the outset, it seemed that the owners were on a mission to destroy their own business—a previously very successful business. There was no communication. The bonus program was taken away. They tried to introduce a daily lunch menu of frozen soups and "sandwiches" that consisted of wispy strips of some kind of meat and about a five-inch-thick, rock hard roll and a thin smear of cheap mayonnaise. They would sit in the bar all day and smoke cigarettes and drink up their booze and profits.

One day, after they had taken away the cell phone stipend, our bonuses, and healthcare, the owner and his wife pull up in a brand new convertible sports car. A few weeks later, they bought an ambulance to pull the giant smoker they had bought. That was actually a pretty cool idea, but it was just the wrong focus and direction. Finally, my time came to an end after I was punched in the face, multiple times in my office, in front of a guest. That was my last straw. My résumé was out in force before the sun rose on the next day.

This time of my life was very stressful and chaotic. I was becoming an Old Salt. A lot of things were happening *to* me. I *felt* like I was making good decisions at the time; and, I had made a series of decisions that probably *were* best for me and my family. I was surrounded by victims of their own stories. I was a victim of mine. Working for people who were never going to be successful, not because they weren't smart or capable, but because they were professionally ignorant, arrogant, insecure and poor leaders.

My time in the bar industry had been a lot of fun and I met a lot of really great people and made great money. But, it was falling apart and family comes first. After discussing things with my wife, we agreed that I should go back to full-service restaurants. So, I polished up the ol' résumé and interviewing skills and jumped in the fray. Soon, I landed a job as Kitchen Manager for a well known Tex Mex food concept. And, unbeknownst to anyone at the time, this led me directly to my first position as GM for a full-service restaurant.

A year after I left the bar, the owners locked the doors. They posted a note on the door and their Facebook page that blamed all of the employees that worked so hard to keep the place afloat. Who knows if they ever looked in the mirror at the real

71

cause of their failure? If they would have stepped back years before and set goals that would have made them successful and taken a problem solving approach instead of using their business as a social outlet, they may have been very successful.

When you are at work, you are in business for yourself. As a server, your three tables are your small business. As a grill cook, your grill and your skill are your revenue generating mechanism. If you allow things to happen _to_ you, your business will not be as successful as it could be if you make things happen _for_ you. In order to do that, you need to have a clear idea of what you can and will contribute, what you want out of work and life, what you need out of work and life, and what people and behaviors are going to help you get there. Then, all you have to do is execute! Simply do it. Sometimes that means getting out of your own way, and having the strength and wisdom to be able to do that can be difficult, and it can be scary.

It is easy to create a vision in your own head where the outcome is failure and then, solely out of *fear*, make the choice not to follow through on the things that would ultimately make you successful. That is only *fear*, and it is to be mastered. Remember, you have the ultimate control.

CHAPTER EIGHT

FLIES AND HONEY

We have touched on relationships a lot so far and there are countless resources available to you to master ways to build better relationships and hold people accountable. So, I am not going to spend a whole lot of time on the *how*, but more the *why*. Once you understand and buy into the concepts discussed in the next couple of pages, then you can go out and spend as much time and money as you want on learning to develop those skills, although it shouldn't take much of either—unless you are a social paraplegic.

First, and this goes along with the making good decisions street in your "Luck/Hard Work Intersection", you must surround yourself with the right people. This is not a one size fits all formula and I do not believe that everyone is essentially good, and I do not have blind faith in the human spirit. There are some flat out shitty people in this world and I believe that there are people

73

who deserve to be shipped off of the planet before they deserve to have a job.

That being said, I *do* believe that all people possess the *ability* to be good, kind and successful, just not necessarily the desire or drive. You are not going to be able to have open accountability conversations with a person who has no desire to help you or to improve themselves or the organization. It is perfectly okay to separate yourself from this person. But, first make certain that you have put in your work and have done everything in your power to build the relationship.

Accountability. This concept is so misinterpreted. I have worked with so many people that believe that accountability has to be written on paper to be successful. Not true. Not even really close to true. Imagine a work environment where everyone got written up for every little thing they did. Can you imagine how miserable everyone would be? Can you imagine how stifled creativity might be as people grow increasingly afraid to make mistakes? I can, because out of frustration and undeveloped leadership skills, I resorted to this tactic once in my career. It was a lot of work for me and everyone was miserable.

You don't have to write someone up every time they cross a line. I have been very successful, especially in the role of department manager, in getting results from people without ever putting pen to paper. Sure, sometimes you have to write people up for things. It shouldn't be your go-to method. Especially considering that you should be practicing accountability skills long before you ever have the position or role-power to write anyone up.

Accountability is a power which any individual can possess, regardless of title, whereby that individual can call upon their knowledge, experience, and personal standards to help themselves or others achieve a higher level of success, understand important information, or redirect behavior toward a common goal of success—through the power of their relationships with others.

That's why strong relationships are so important. Self-accountability is easy. All you have to do is do it, right? Hold yourself accountable. No problem! You'd think it was the hardest thing to do on Earth based on the apparent lack of self-accountability practiced by even the most powerful members of our society. But try holding someone else accountable to a standard you have is even more difficult, especially if they don't know you, don't respect you, or flat out hate you.

When you take the time to develop meaningful relationships with people and become masterful at asking for, and following up on, the things and behaviors you need or want, accountability gets so much easier. Each person is unique, and so must your approach be with them. Also, the difficulty level varies from person to person, job to job, and situation to situation.

When you are trying to master accountability it is important to remember the human element. Never let frustration or anger be the basis for your discussions because you can damage the relationship, sometimes irreparably. It doesn't matter who was right or wrong in accountability. Pointing fingers is not going to get you anywhere. It's about being able to master the ability to have conversations about missed expectations without being upset or making the other person feel inadequate or disrespected. I'm not saying it is easy, it's not. But with practice, you can do it.

Try thinking of something you need from a friend. Maybe you are a nonsmoker and your friend always smokes around you. It bothers you, and you wish she would stop. Try this. Say, "Aimee, can I ask you something?"

Being your dear friend, she will undoubtedly say something like, "Sure."

"It really bothers me a lot when you smoke around me, can we talk about a way that you can continue smoking but let's me stay smoke free? I'd really appreciate it."

Aimee will probably agree and a conversation will ensue. There is a chance that one of you may become insulted, angry or frustrated. Just remember that your friends and preserving the relationship is the most important thing. That doesn't mean Aimee gets to smoke whenever she wants, and it doesn't mean you get to dictate when or where she does. Hopefully, you both understand the consequences of not reaching a mutually beneficial solution to this. You could lose the friendship!

I am not sure how many of you all know smokers, but now imagine having that conversation with someone who doesn't like you. I have seen people get cut for less.

My Grandmother also used to tell me, "You always catch more flies with honey than you do with vinegar."

To which my Grandfather would quip, "What about manure?"

Well, hopefully you get the point.

CHAPTER NINE

DON'T BE (DELIBERATELY) OBTUSE

That phrase got Andy Dufresne in some pretty hot water in The Shawshank Redemption and being deliberately obtuse will piss your team and your boss off faster than you can blink.

First off, acute and obtuse are antonyms. Acute means sharp, obtuse means wide, or in this case dull (or dumb).

I used to have a manager who worked for me. His way of letting me know he was unhappy with a work assignment was that he would play dumb. He would take my instructions very literally and then when he ultimately failed to achieve his goal he would split hairs and say things like, "well, you said…" Very annoying.

He did the same thing with his team when they would approach him with concerns, or needs. He would try to trick them into contradicting themselves and then almost celebrate when he caught them in the contradiction. It caused a lot of stress for them. It was a very condescending way of showing his self-perceived mental superiority. In the year and a half this manager worked for me, he literally did not see one single project through to completion. He went out of his way to make his job and mine more difficult. This guy used to be a GM for another restaurant company, too, and it just baffled me that he was so unproductive and obtuse. He built roadblocks for himself and everyone else he worked with.

You have to be flexible and you have to use a little common sense. You will receive instructions and if your boss is being too specific, or not specific enough, then you really just need to know ways that you can communicate that in a way that shows you understand the goal and what the final outcome should be. Then, *reach the final outcome.*

If you show yourself as a person who cannot be mentally flexible and as someone who would rather play dumb to prove a point then you are not representing your value to the organization well.

A common excuse for failure to meet basic expectations also happens to be "I'm sorry, I didn't know." Sometimes this is legit, a lot of times it's crap, or it's your own fault for not knowing. Whether because you weren't paying attention, sharp or experienced enough to see the desired end result, or you did not care; none of those excuses holds a lot of water in my book, except for lack of experience. The other excuses? At best they paint you as an airhead, and at worst it makes you look like a complete uncooperative idiot. Don't sell yourself short, and certainly never give me or anyone else a reason to.

Get used to the word "and". It is funny to me that people can look at two independently good ideas as conflicting. For example, achieving lower labor goals AND being fully staffed for every shift. Or, hitting your food cost goal AND being vigilant about quality food and plate presentations. Presenting yourself to your boss as a person who sees these things as OR statements instead of AND statements will make your job very stressful, and it will not be a very flattering reflection when review time comes around. "And" is a good word. I always tell my teams, "I am a cake AND eat it too kind of guy".

Pay attention. Use common sense. If something is important to your boss, you'd better damn well make it important to yourself. And, if you think it is clever to intentionally play dumb to get a point across then reevaluate your commitment to being a professional. Being deliberately obtuse is annoying, childish, it's a waste of time, and it is decidedly unprofessional.

CHAPTER TEN

CHOOSE YOUR BLOOD TYPE, B+ OR B-

"Courage is resistance to fear, mastery of fear, not absence of fear."—Mark Twain

"Efforts and courage are not enough without purpose and direction."—John F. Kennedy

One of the reasons that I am writing this book is that I had such a hard time figuring out what it takes to be a leader. The whole concept was shrouded in mystery. I confused leadership with simply being in charge for the longest time. A good leader must be able to take charge, certainly, but the tools you have at your disposal to do so are the true components of leadership. It took me a long time to sort that out. My hope is that I can remove some of that mystery, and make the transition for you a much simpler process.

There is another reason I am writing this book. It is a more personal reason, and why I chose the quotes above and—incidentally—why it took me so long to advance in my career. That reason is that I have a very powerful temper. I feel things very personally, and intensely. I love with my whole heart, and I can hate with every ounce of my soul. I am a very passionate person. This has served me well, and it has also hindered me immensely. Terrible things happened to me in my childhood and I brought those things with me to adulthood, for a time. Negative thoughts challenged me and tripped me up almost every day of my life, personally and professionally.

I wasted a lot of time wondering why me? I wallowed in self pity wondering why bad things always seemed to happen to me. I watched other people get ahead; meanwhile, I was ready with a sarcastic comment. People would pass me by for promotions, meanwhile I'd have all the armchair-CEO reasons why that decision was wrong and why the person would fail, and why I'd have done things better. I was piling up roadblocks in front of myself left and right as fast as I could.

My temper cost me my first marriage as well as other relationships that may have been mutually fruitful. I caused myself a great deal of distress. Remember, at the age of nineteen I got in a fight that cost me my freedom for a time. I missed many career advancement opportunities because of my inability to cope with anger, confrontation, frustration, and failure. And it was *always* someone else's fault. Then, I began to recognize a trend. Of *all* the different problems I had, of *all* the unique and terrible circumstances I encountered, there was only one common thread—me.

Maybe that sounds like common sense to you. I hope so. For me it was more like a full blown epiphany! It was like a lightning bolt straight to a secret part of the brain that only wakes up when God is talking. I was so blinded by my roadblocks—past experiences, acquired habits based in those bad experiences, old excuses, and negativity, that I couldn't see all the harm that I was causing myself. It was that drunken, rainy November night full of self-pity and self-loathing when I was shown four immeasurably important things:

1. There are a lot of really great gifts in my life that I should appreciate and be grateful for.

2. The past happened and it is gone and there is not a damn thing I can do about it now.

3. If I am going to be a better person, I need to focus on the future and rid myself of the negative influences in my life—both external and self-imposed.

4. I need to change the things that I can, and stop worrying about the things that I cannot.

I became so painfully aware of how self centered and arrogant I had been wallowing in my problems and living in the past. The next day I took two actions that had an immediate positive impact on my life.

First, I eliminated the people from my life that I felt were always negative. I literally broke up with some of them, and I simply quit associating with others.

Second, I began changing the way I thought about things. Easier said than done, but I made an intense effort to frame every thought I had in a positive light—no matter how negative the situation.

Later on I did seemingly silly stuff like look myself in the face every day and say something nice about myself, I started finding a way to compliment everyone I talked to no matter how brief the interaction. Arguments and confrontations became much more interesting as the first thing I tried to do was to *listen* and reflect the other person's point of view as I understood it, before expressing my viewpoint. I made a concerted effort not to complain about anything, ever. Of no small importance, I also began making better decisions! Decisions were consciously weighed against my goals and morals and my vision for me. My life's mission statement if you will.

Look, I wasn't then, nor am I now, perfect at any of these things, but I have gotten pretty damn good, and continuous improvement is a personal value. I strive to get a little better each day. Maybe this sounds self centered to you, but if you think about it in commercial aviation terms, you must affix your own mask in the event of an emergency before you attempt to help anyone else.

Folks, I have already written about this, but it is worth repeating: The positive changes in my life were immediate and dramatic. Positive relationships in my life flourished. I developed life-long and unbreakable friendships. I met my wife. My career and income advanced exponentially.

Steven Covey talks about Positive Mental Attitude, or PMA, in his book The Seven Habits of Highly Effective People (read it) and how it can impact the world around you. There is no purer case of success with this concept than my experience.

My lightning bolt, my battle with God and my Demons, was intense and long lived. When it was over, it was as if someone flipped a switch and I became an entirely different human, and the experience was liberating. When you finally realize how much control you have over yourself and the things that happen for you, you are truly free to remove your roadblocks at will.

You have a choice, and do not delude or delay yourself by disagreeing with that statement. If you disagree with the statement, put the book down for a while and think about the reaction you have had to the last three negative circumstances in your life. Each time, for better or worse, you chose how to respond.

Each day you make the choice to interact with your world in a positive way, or a negative way. Remember, no neutral energy. You get back what you put into it. Garbage in, garbage out—so to speak. I heard a saying once, "If you smile, the world will smile back at you". I believe deeply that this is true.

Now, I am not saying that if you are super positive all the time that you will never face adversity. That is foolish to take from any of this, and decidedly untrue. Adversity is a big part of life, as are confrontation and failure. You have to decide how you are going to deal with these things. You can choose to be overcome by these things, or you can choose to stand up to these things. You will *need* to fight in your life. You will fail in your life. When you do, do so with a warrior's heart and a smile on your face; and, learn something from each experience—no matter how horrible the circumstances. It will make your victories much more swift and rewarding.

One of the greatest pitfalls that I have seen people fall into is thinking that because they are great at their jobs, that this somehow entitles them to be as negative as they like about things. These people often feel as if they are doing the organization a service by constantly pointing out all of the things that are wrong, and they should be respected for speaking their mind. They may frequently share all of their opinions with team members and probably spend a lot of time griping about the way they would do things if they were in charge. These folks are always in someone's ear about the negative and rarely mention anything positive.

Hey, again folks, I have been this guy. I understand where you are coming from. Chances are, you are right about a lot of the things you observe. I try to take myself back to that time of my life and get inside my own head and try and remember my motivation. I believe even to this day, that I had the company's best interest at heart, but I had no real skill in channeling my energy in a positive way and disagreeing or bringing up my concerns in a positive way.

Further, I had even less of a clue how to impact the team with solutions rather than just bitching about all of the problems. I was also *very* good at the technical side of my job. In fact, I was the best at it by any measurement in a very large company—which probably saved my ass a few times. Luckily, I had a great manager who I respected and was able to help me see the way my negative attitude (which I did not see as negative at the time, by the way) affected those around me.

You may see yourself as passionate, intense, and knowledgeable. But, if you are the one who is constantly finding fault and trying to "fix" the problem by spreading the gospel of negativity, then—and your boss may not put it this way to you, so

I am going to take a burden from his or her shoulders and just lay it out there for you—you are being an asshole. Knock it off. If you think that you are the only person that is aware of the problem, chances are you are also being short sighted and arrogant.

Mangers, contrary to popular belief, are actually human beings. They are capable of making mistakes, and we do not have all of the answers. To truly be valuable to the organization takes much more than being technically proficient, and aware of problems. You must be understanding and be a positive person who is willing to see the company, and your boss, through the tough times and help provide solutions that have a positive impact on your team and the organization. And as painful as it may be to those of us who suffer from instant-gratificationism, cool your jets and be patient and be consistent.

Wars are won through a long series of intense battles, some of which you will win and some of which you will lose. Don't give up and carefully choose your battles, and (more importantly) how you fight them, and you and your whole team will win in the end.

What does this sound like? Well, if you have ever heard yourself or anyone else say things that sound like any of the following, then be careful because you are displaying attributes of B-Negative blood type:

"Idiots."

"Why can't they see this problem?"

"If I ran this place, I would do this!"

"Can you believe this crap?"

"Screw this job/manager/place."

All of these come in vastly different forms ranging from menacing silence to profane aggressive outbursts or statements and even walking out on the job.

Remember this: Negativity breeds negativity, aggression breeds aggression and, positivity breeds positivity. It is very literally <u>your</u> decision how you choose to interact with the world and those around you. And, it starts inside your head. Relax a little. If things are that bad, then quit! Go find a job where you will be happy. When you realize that you are unhappy from place to place to place though, you have to be ready to accept that you are the common denominator.

Make good decisions. Change the way you think about problems and difficult people or circumstances. Challenge yourself before you challenge others. Have positive purpose and direction in your day to day encounters and activities.

In a later chapter, we will talk about how to Feed Your Egg and become a Solution Based Thinker. For now, focus on making sure that you have a B-Positive blood type. Your success in life and at work greatly depends on your ability to contribute value to the respective worlds around you.

Positive people do this naturally. For others, it can be very difficult. Yet, it is a skill that can be learned. Once you train yourself to think in a positive way and to contribute positive energy, solutions, and results consistently, then you dramatically increase your value to those you serve.

I want to end this chapter with two more quotes, and please understand that my selections relating to courage and character are in no way unintentional or misplaced. True self-improvement takes immense courage, and boatloads of character.

"Watch your thoughts, they become words. Watch your words, they become actions. Watch your actions, they become habits. Watch your habits, they become character. Watch your character, it becomes your destiny."—Lao Tzu

"Courage is being scared to death, and saddling up anyway."—John Wayne

PART TWO

APTITUDE

CHAPTER ELEVEN

THE "HOW-TO" RULE OF TOOLS AND SELF-DEVELOPMENT

You are going to be shown a lot of things throughout your career. You will probably read a lot of books. It is going to be tempting to take everything you read at face value and you will drive yourself up the wall trying to take everything so literally. I am not going to give you a lot of rules in this book, but in this chapter I give you one: *Learn How to Customize Tools to <u>Your</u> Situation.*

I don't care what author you read, no matter what their experience is or how much research they have done, the ideas they put forth in their books (including this one) are just that—ideas. They are opinions and perspective. You'd go nuts trying to apply all of the things that have worked for me in my life to yours if you did so step by step and word for word! I am not you. You are not me. What worked for me may work for you, but you have to make it yours. Make it *sound* like you. It is easy to take advice in books like this very literally and get wrapped up in all the reasons that the idea won't work for you.

If this is you, then take a step back from the tool (this book in this case) and reevaluate what you hope to achieve. The journey of self-development that you have embarked on is a painstakingly slow process. There is no magic bullet that is going to miraculously transform you over night.

Most likely, you will only occasionally pick up pieces of information that make an immediate difference in your thoughts and behaviors and have a great impact in your day to day life. But for the most part, you aren't going to read a book and think and act differently the next day. Take away a few useful tidbits of information and use them. Collect them from various sources. Mash them all up and see what happens. Experiment. Teach them to others.

When you get good at that or find a way that works well for you, go revisit some old books and ideas and see if you get something new out of them. You have to think a bit abstractly and have the mental flexibility to see how the ideas being conveyed by the author are useful to you in your situation.

You are always going to view any material through the lens of necessity. That is, if you are struggling with something—

say, accountability—everything you see will be viewed through that lens. When you improve at accountability, and you reread something with another focus—say coaching and motivation—you are likely to get something completely different out of it. It's all about perspective. As your collection grows and you improve your skills of self-development, it really gets quite exciting.

I will use the book *Good to Great*, by Jim Collins as an example. It's relatively high level stuff. A good read, although really packed full of information that I really didn't need—or want—as a reader the first time I read it. It is also geared toward an executive audience. I am not an executive, but on the advice of the president of my company I had to take myself out of my GM role and promote myself to CEO of my fifty person corporation.

The value of certain lessons in that book is immeasurable. Many people have probably heard one of the key lessons in that book regurgitated thousands of times, but it paints the perfect picture. That is the "Bus Analogy". Making sure I had the right people on my bus was my first order of business after I finished that book. When I re-read it, I am sure it will have a much different impact.

Continuous self-improvement is an absolute necessity. If you think you are good enough, congratulations! Retire. The rest of your life will be pretty dull, and your career is essentially over anyway. I do not know a single professional that isn't constantly searching for ways to improve themselves, sharpen an existing skill, or learn something new. Stephen Covey calls this "Sharpening the Saw".

CHAPTER TWELVE

ORGANIZATION AND TIME MANAGEMENT

This chapter isn't for everyone; maybe you are great at organization and managing your time. Good for you! Maybe you spend way too much time trying to be organized and need to relax a bit. Maybe you think you suck at it but are really pretty good, that was the case with me.

Once, I reached out to some colleagues and asked for some guidance relating to this. They asked what system I used, so I explained it to them. They all essentially laughed at me and said I was fine. One well respected Proprietor in our organization said, "Dude, you do more than I do!" The confidence that this feedback gave me was all I needed to remove this from my pile of roadblocks and move forward.

Maybe you really are terrible at it. And that's okay. This is a perfect example of a self-inflicted roadblock and it just takes a desire to improve and remarkably little discipline. Again, there are a TON of books and seminars out there. You can spend a lot of money if you want to pick up some tips and tricks, but you really don't need to do that.

It's really pretty easy. You don't need a planner, although it doesn't hurt to have some sort of calendar. This is one of those situations where you should look for ways to make it your own, but here is my way: I use a pocket card holder, a spiral bound notebook, legal pad and a leather pad-folio with one pocket and my smart phone. It doesn't have to be expensive, fancy or elaborate.

Remember, remove your own roadblocks. Ready? Okay.

Successful organization and time management really boils down to a few basic elements.

1. Developing a simple system.

2. Developing a routine around the system.

3. Holding yourself accountable to executing the routine.

That's it. It can be as unique or typical as you like. You can steal from someone else if you want. Don't overcomplicate it. If you make the choice to ignore number 3, it won't work. Simple as that. No amount of developing your system will be worth more than a pile of paper on your desk if you choose not to do anything with it.

The three previous points hinge on this concept: Make it easy and make it happen.

I remember when I was younger I'd spend a ton of money on fancy day planners and PDA units and they were all junk. None of them worked nearly as good as my plain old yellow legal pad for one reason, I never used it. I use my notebook all the time. I just like the look and feel of pen to paper. I can scribble and doodle and jot my thoughts down as they come. I developed my system around that knowledge of myself.

Here's how I work the routine and my system:

1. I have my pocket card holder that I stock with fresh 3x5 index cards as needed. I use this to jot down names or other important things that happen throughout my day that I need to remember. This may include R&M issues, Team Member requests, etc.

2. I have a master task/idea list that these cards get "dumped" onto. I refer to this list throughout my day, but I always start my day by scouring the list for items that must be completed. These urgent items are marked with an "A" or a star in the left-hand margin and are the first ones to be crossed off of my list. Time sensitive items have the due date written beside them. After all of my A/star priorities are crossed off, I pick new ones, and

A/star those. As I check emails in the office, I have this pad sitting next to me so that action items find their way onto the list immediately. When my list gets to two or three pages, I tear them off and rewrite it. That's about every three days.

3. Important dates go into my smart phone calendar with appropriate reminders set an hour, a day, or a week in advance depending on why and when I need to be reminded.

4. In the spiral bound notebook is where I keep my notes from every meeting I have. Whether it is a manager one-on-one or a sit down with a Team Member, I take notes. I keep those notes in files I keep on each person so that I can refer to them later if I need to.

That's all there is to it. I use Outlook to a lesser extent. I use that more to remind my management team when there is an action item I want them to take care of. This system helps me stay on task, get things done, remember things and most importantly, it frees up my mind to focus on other things. If you rely on your brain (however smart you may be) to keep track of your day to day tasks, ideas and plans, you will forget things and your planning time will not be as productive as you struggle to remember all the things you need to do. The more successful you become, the more things you will have on your plate, and the more necessary strict discipline to execute such a system becomes. Also, be flexible. I can only imagine that my system will evolve in some unpredictable ways as I progress in my career.

One word of caution, you can easily become obsessed and spend a lot of time trying to be more organized. This will equate to lost time. A good system is one that is not only effective, but easy and efficient. It only has to work for you. Remember, the most important time you spend is spent developing relationships with the people around you, not nitpicking over the format of your calendar.

CHAPTER THIRTEEN

FEED YOUR EGG: A TRICK TO HELP WITH SOLUTION-BASED THINKING

Problems, problems, problems! We are all faced with problems. Every day, day in and day out we deal with problems. Problems with a team member, problems with supply, problems with labor and production, problems with guests, facilities, supplies, coworkers, equipment, the list can go on and on.

How often do you see people address a problem with more problems? I can think of an example I experienced at my bank. A check had not been put into our positive pay check system and was therefore not payable, meaning that I would be without change in the restaurant for the day. Previous tellers at the same bank had been able to force the system to accept the check in the past, so I asked for this service again. It was our fault, the closing manager had not entered the check like he was supposed to, and I didn't double check it that morning like I was supposed to. But I needed help, so I asked.

The new bank manager came over and explained in excruciating detail how he was unable to help me, even after I had explained that the previous manager had done it for me recently. He spent an impressive amount of time detailing the problems he faced in making this happen, rather than spend even a second discussing possible solutions, and providing me with a possible solution to my problem. He absolutely fumbled a great hospitality moment.

Maybe you have faced a problem you didn't know how to solve recently. A very common thing for people who are inexperienced at problem solving to do is to immediately become combative or defensive when presented with an issue. A natural tendency is to want to shift blame to others, or to situations that really have no purpose in the discussion, thus creating more problems.

So, if you are a person who struggles with this, I have created an exercise to help you. It is called Feeding the Egg, and it comes with a delightfully cheesy analogy. So here we go.

Imagine that you are a hen about to lay an egg. As a proud mama chicken, you are tasked with solving a problem, and that is how to lay a healthy egg that grows into a self-sufficient chicken, free to roam and peck and cluck and hopefully raise a brood of its own. You have to eat right to form a strong shell and make sure your little egg develops, and then once it's laid you have to keep it warm, and protect it from raccoons. If you are not careful and provide adequate nourishment, your egg's shell could become brittle, or the embryo inside could become malnourished or cold and die.

That isn't what we want. We want a healthy chicken. So everything we give it is going to be nourishing. Healthy food, warmth, shelter, love. First, I want you to think of a problem that needs solved. Let's say you have been asked in a one-on-one with a manager to improve your per person check average.

Now, draw an egg shape in the middle of a blank sheet of paper. In the center of the egg, write your desired outcome, in this case "Improved PPA". Now, draw four or five arrows pointing into the egg. Now on each one of these lines write a specific action step that would help you solve your problem. The only rule is that if you come up with something for any of the lines that requires more than one action, it gets its own egg. The idea is to get to the simplest solution.

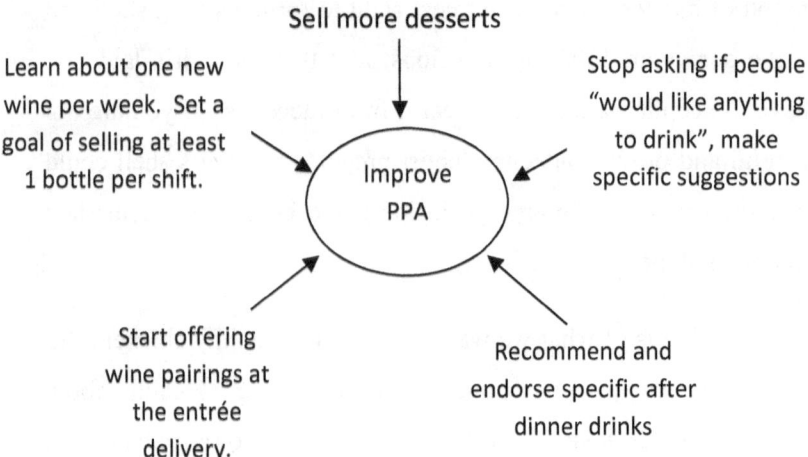

Sell more desserts

Learn about one new wine per week. Set a goal of selling at least 1 bottle per shift.

Improve PPA

Stop asking if people "would like anything to drink", make specific suggestions

Start offering wine pairings at the entrée delivery.

Recommend and endorse specific after dinner drinks

In the diagram you see specific actions listed that could potentially lead to an increased check average. If you look at the top item, however, this is not a specific action. You could break "Sell More Desserts" into a whole new category with its own solutions. In essence, you have added another problem to your list. I recommend replacing that with something that has more value, such as, "Specifically endorse a different dessert to each table focusing on enticing verbiage".

This brings me to the important difference between goals and actions. Actions are not goals, and goals are not actions. A **goal** (as defined by me) is a desired end result not currently held or achieved that is supported by a group of consistently executed existing or new behaviors, or **actions**. This group of actions is known as the **action plan**. The trick is executing the plan. SPOILER ALERT: There is not much of a trick to it.

After Feeding Your Egg, your action plan might look something like this:

Goal:

Improve PPA from $19.00 to $20.00 per person average by (1 month) through enhanced wine and bar beverage knowledge and service.

Benefit:

Increased checks = higher total sales = more tip money = (personal reward i.e., new car)

People Involved/Follow up:

Me, FOH manager (per shift), GM (per week)

Tools Needed:

Tracking spreadsheet, wine tasting notes, wine passport, wine key, GUMPTION and TENACITY! ☺

Actions:

• Begin offering specific and tailored after dinner drinks to each table. Coffee, Gran Marnier, Dessert Wine, Port. Timeframe—Immediately. Follow up with FOH manager each shift.

- Learn about 1 new wine per week and sell one bottle per shift. Tasting and training with FOH manager. Timeframe—Beginning of the first shift of each week.

- Begin offering specific wine pairings with each entrée at the delivery. Timeframe—immediately. Discuss techniques, successes and failures with FOH manager 5 minutes each shift.

- Remove the phrase "would you care for anything to drink" from my vocabulary. Replace with specific drink recommendations and endorsements. Timeframe—immediately. Follow up on each shift with FOH manager.

- Offer wine samples of my newly learned wines to people who are on the fence as a way to secure my knowledge and create hospitality. Timeframe—Immediately. Follow up each shift with FOH manager.

- Sit down with GM 1x per week to discuss successes and opportunities, and to see how I am performing to my goal.

- Meet or exceed my goal to increase PPA by $1 in one month. Discuss in final weekly meeting with GM.

Notice that most of these actions turn out to be things you can do right away. Notice that most, if not all, of the ownership lies with you, and you merely follow up with your support team to help keep yourself on track. No one is doing any of this for you. As you go through your career, these types of things will get much more complex, and you won't need this simplistic tool, but the principle is the same. Set a goal, figure out what tools, people, and actions you need to achieve it, and by when—and then do it.

The idea is that as you become more and more accustomed to thinking in this way of simplifying problems to the core actions that lead to improvement, you easily reach a point where you need to rely on this tool less and less. It is simply the way you think now. And, guess what? You have just increased your value to the organization.

CHAPTER FOURTEEN

GOAL SETTING

Goal setting can be intimidating. I recently had the pleasure, of working with an executive job coach. I was a nervous wreck! I had all kinds of inflated ideas about what it would be like. I had a huge complicated vision of things.

Simply put, I was wrong. It was really simple but it wasn't easy. There were lots of long hard looks in the mirror. I had to accept that the way I had been doing certain things was not helping me, and learn to recognize roadblocks that I had been constructing for myself. It was very painful in some ways.

In the end, I was able to set four challenging goals for my self-development and I achieved my goals at a high level. It was very exciting. The most exciting part of this was that I could take what I was learning and immediately apply the principles to my daily job, and share them with the people I am mentoring and watch them use them. You can do it too. Learning to master yourself and then teaching others to do the same is extremely invigorating. Leadership is as much about hospitality as anything else. You have to have a genuine concern for others and a strong desire to help others be successful.

Deciding what you want to do is pretty easy. I have a couple of rules for you about goal setting.

1. Never set a goal that you can achieve too easily. It is great to cross things off a list, but if you aren't stretching beyond your comfort zone, you aren't growing. You are simply crossing items off a checklist.

2. Don't set goals that are too difficult to reach. If the goal is overwhelming you, and you have a hard time getting going, you have maybe set your sights too high. Start slow and small at first and build your goal achieving muscle as you get more experience.

3. Pick things that have real world impact and achieve measureable results. Measureable can be tricky. It is hard to quantify certain things like attitude improvement or coaching ability. Be creative, because if you look at the results, you can easily measure certain things. You just have to look at the impact that your improvement of a particular skill or trait will have.

Sometimes you may have to separate by a couple of degrees, but the impact is there and measureable.

4.   Write it down and share it with someone who can help you achieve your results.   Pick a person, or mentor, who has experience in setting and achieving goals and ask them to help you edit your list.

5.   Do not confuse tasks for goals.   Tasks could very well be part of your action planning, but a task is not a goal.   Task completion is a very important part of your job, but all you ever do is check tasks off a list, you are not going to achieve your goals. You need to know where you are going to end up.   Your goal is your destination and a well written action plan is your map.

6.   Do it.   Be aggressive.   Even if you aren't totally sure what you are doing.   As you develop as a leader in this business you are going to have a lot of opportunities to do new things.   So, you will be doing things you aren't familiar with.   Do not be afraid to make mistakes.   Mistakes are good teachers.   Just try not to make the same one twice and you are good to go.

The difference between a goal and a task is pretty simple. This is kind of like the Feed Your Egg model.   The difference might look like this:

Task: I will hold a class on wine for the front of house team to improve their knowledge and help them increase sales.

Goal: I will increase wine sales by 3% over the current average of 4.5% by January 1st, 2014.

Do you see the difference?   The first example is a very good idea, and beneficial to your team, but it is simply a step in the process toward achieving the goal outlined in the second example.

Executed properly, the second goal should have multiple steps, or tasks, that need to be accomplished in order to be achieved.   Other steps might include things like setting up a tracking sheet to track the numbers of bottles sold per day, creating a contest, making a wine passport that servers can get signed off on by management. The list could be as extensive or as simple as you want, or as required by the goal. It's not rocket science. Don't roadblock yourself by making it too complicated. Most problems, or goals, have simple, logical and chronological solutions. Action and follow up are usually the missing pieces.

Ken Blanchard's leadership training uses a model called S.M.A.R.T. Goals.   S.M.A.R.T. stands for Specific and Measureable, Motivating, Attainable, Relevant, and Trackable and Timebound.   This is an excellent model to use to measure the validity of your goals. And, I recommend getting your hands on as much Blanchard material as possible. It's effective and simple and a really good place to start

111

Again, as you go into this for the first time, a mentor can be a valuable partner for helping you stay on track and motivated. It is easy to get discouraged when you don't know what you are doing. Being outside your comfort zone can be really scary and really exhausting. Do not give up! When you feel that stress and exhaustion, that is when you need to dig deep and push a little harder. Soon, you will grab the brass ring. There are not many better feelings in life than setting a lofty goal and then achieving it. As you get better at it, you can set higher and higher bars, and as you achieve those higher and higher goals, the feeling soon becomes addictive.

After you set a goal, the action plan comes into play. Break the goal down into basic and achievable steps. Feed Your Egg. The solutions you come up with in the Feed Your Egg model are the steps in your action plan. Organize them in the most sensible chronological order, and execute the plan. It is not enough just to check the items off of your list. You need to have *honest* check-ins with yourself about how successful you were with each step. Maybe you are not happy with how your wine class went. Okay, now what? You can make adjustments to the plan at any stage of the game. Keep it simple, though, and don't change things around too much, but if you feel you missed the mark on something then try to find a way to revisit that step and get better results.

For example, let's say that you have held the wine class for your front of house team and you are seeing that some, or all, of the knowledge you tried to impart on your team seems to have escaped a few people. It happens. This is a great opportunity to spend some one-on-one time with the team members who are struggling to find out what you can do differently to help them feel successful in this area.

Notice the focus on what _you_ can do differently. You are the leader, so the responsibility falls upon you to tailor your approach. Sure, they have to meet you half way in some respects, but leadership and training is not a one size fits all model. Getting the best results from people is not easy, and it takes time and experience to get really good at motivating people and getting truly good at holding people accountable. Trust me, we all wish it was. But as Dad used to say, "You can wish in one hand...". Well, I will let you imagine how that analogy ends—but its gross.

Follow up and follow through should be part of your routine anyway. The point is, it's not enough just to dump information on your team and expect them to own it. It is your responsibility to help it take hold, and you do that by consistent follow up and measuring their levels of success.

The saying goes, what gets measured, gets done. If you only take one thing away from this chapter, please take this: An action plan without the action is simply a dusty page on a shelf somewhere.

113

CHAPTER FIFTEEN

GET IT DONE...NOW!

Leadership comes from within, and you must demonstrate leadership far before you ever become a manager or move up in your career. Responsibility is granted to those who demonstrate ability before they are promoted. You will never get the rewards you seek if you have the mentality that you will not execute until you are paid to do so. It's just not how the world works.

If you expect a high level of achievement from yourself, your team and your peers, they will be more likely to achieve it. If you wait to get things off of your plate, you will always be behind. Organizations value people who can stay on top of their job, and take on more happily and willingly. Why wait? Be a person that things happen for. No matter what obstacles are in your path, rise to the challenge and surmount it.

Look, this is really pretty easy. Your reputation as a task manager isn't the *most* important, but it is still *very* important. You have to be able to get things done. Being a good leader of people is an extremely valuable trait, but it is only half the battle. You have responsibilities, too. My advice: If your boss gives you a task or project to be done tomorrow, be the person who gets it done today.

"How do I do that?" you ask.

Nike said it best, "Just do it."

Assuming that you and I are on the same page in regards to "mistakes" referring to fixable missteps and not inadvertently burning down the building…don't be afraid of making mistakes.

Carelessness, Neglect, and Accident are not too far removed from one another. You break a glass because you are careless. You lose a customer because you neglected to follow up effectively. You carelessly cause an accident because you neglected to look behind you before you turn around. When one of my kids would break something or knock something over, I'd get after them about it, and they'd say "Well I didn't mean too!" To which I would always say, "Well, you didn't mean not to either." They *loved* that.

Mistake is a totally different word. Another dumb play on words from yours truly? Don't mind if I do!

115

The word mistake might suggest that you *took* the time to consider the outcome of your actions, and *missed*. A mistake is easy to forgive. Neglect and carelessness can be more difficult.

Jump in with both feet, thoughtfully. The worst *mistake* you can make is not getting it done. If your boss is worth a damn, he or she will understand that people screw up, and will also understand that it isn't the end of the world. To be fair, they are quite justified in expecting that you do not make the same error again. Valuable people learn and grow from their past experiences. And, if there is a mistake looming that you just aren't comfortable making—ask questions!

CHAPTER SIXTEEN

TEAMWORK

This is a pretty simple concept. It is much easier after you have truly challenged your own thoughts and actions and have begun to view yourself as a positive person and contributor.

The cliché is that there is no "I" in team.

Well, there isn't, but I disagree with the spirit of the statement. Successful teamwork is not about you or any other individual. It is about the results that you produce as a team, right? Again, very true, but I will challenge the cliché in one important way. Each member of the team should always be thinking things like:

"How can **I** contribute to our success today?"

"What can **I** do to help others around me?"

"Which team members can **I** help be stronger contributors?"

"What will **I** learn today, and how will **I** use that knowledge to help the team?"

"How can **I** be better today than **I** was yesterday?"

"What role am **I** best at to help the team achieve success?"

You get the point I hope. You have to think about your own contributions and what you can do to be better. But this is where the cliché comes into play. The end result is not about you. It is about being aware of your contribution to the greater good, and improving your contribution. Teamwork is a **selfless** devotion of your knowledge and your skills, abilities, talents, and work ethic to a group with a common vision or goal.

As a member of any team you are going to be surrounded by individuals who are not as good as you are in some aspects of your job. Chances are, you work in close proximity to someone who is better than you at something important. You will be, unfortunately, working in close proximity to a few individuals who do not care as much as you do

Inevitably you will absorb work that is not done by these individuals, and this can appear unfair—if you look at it in the wrong light. The world, by its own design, is not populated with billions of equals (sorry Jefferson). Some people are better than others at certain things. You have a choice to make here and it can be guided by the selfless principles of teamwork. You can get wrapped up in the "fairness", or you can continue to give everything you have each day to contribute to the success of the team. Chances are that at some point in your career, somebody picked up your slack and helped you become stronger, too. It is really easy to tear someone down who isn't as strong as you are. It is very rewarding to raise that person up instead.

Ultimately, do you really want your success to hinge upon the actions or inactions of other people? No. Develop your own sense of teamwork and live it consistently and passionately and set the example, and I promise that those around you will strive to meet you at your level. They may fall short of your standards— and, get over yourself. Even if they fall short, they will certainly be higher than they were, and you should recognize their improvement and respect it. The ones that don't care will leave, or change. Don't let them hold you down, try to raise them up. At the end of the day, they may never be as good as you are, but your dedication to upholding your own values and work ethic will at some level impact them and make them better.

It is easy to get discouraged when you work on a team where not all the pieces fit together. As a team member, work hard to develop a core group of like minded individuals and continuously reach out to those falling short. Never give up. As a manger, be very aware of who you choose to place on your team and be very alert, and react quickly when you make a bad choice. Listen to your core contributing team members, they will let you know.

When you are an effective team, you are unstoppable. Constant and open communication is critical! You have to be open to the criticism of your peers. You have to own your mistakes and share your victories. Seek to own blame and dispense praise. You have to be able to discuss failures without casting personal dispersions and negativity.

George McKerrow, Jr., a man whom I look up to in business; and, a leader that I have had the unmatched privilege and pleasure of working for in my career, can be heard saying as often as he gets the chance, "We all look good together, and we all look bad together."

Remember: Leadership is not a title, it is a quality. Understanding and executing true teamwork and team commitment is a critical part of leadership.

CHAPTER SEVENTEEN

PRODUCT EXCELLENCE

One of the most dangerous pitfalls in business is uncontrolled costs. You can flush a bunch of money right down the toilet before you even knew it was there. In my opinion, it is equally dangerous to control costs too much.

What I mean is, never sacrifice quality for price.

I think we've all done it. It's easy. You are under immense pressure. The wheels are coming off and things are out of control, you have to move and you are needed five other places. You look at a plate of food and you make a decision. As soon as it leaves your hands, you feel that twinge of guilt and shame. You know you shouldn't have sent it. You know that it wasn't right, but you are busy. It happens. The biggest problem is: Ten other people just watched you do it. You just let them know that it was ok to sacrifice quality for time or money.

What is arguably much worse, though, is when you intentionally send inferior product to the table as a method of controlling food cost. Just don't do it. If sending a crappy product to a table as a method of cost control is your business model, then I will give you a simple formula for figuring your food cost below.

30% (Cost of Goods Sold) x $0.00 (Sales) = $0.00

You will have nothing to worry about. You will be run out of business, and rightfully so. There is plenty of other low hanging fruit in your business that you can choose from to control costs. Never sacrifice the integrity of your product to make the P&L. Do it, and you cut your own throat. You have no one else to blame for your failure but yourself.

If you consistently offer excellent products, educate and lead your team with sincere hospitality and offer your product at a fair price, you will almost certainly be fine.

CHAPTER EIGHTEEN

TRAINING AND DEVELOPMENT

The ability to train and to teach others is quite possibly the most important skill you will ever learn. Mastering the skill of training early in your career will shape your ability to achieve results from your teams throughout your career. This skill will not only serve you well professionally—but personally as you begin to raise your children. This book is designed to teach you all of the little things that are important about training. I could write an entire book about that alone. But, I will bullet point some very important concepts for you:

- You are the first impression of the company's culture. Always make your trainees feel welcome in every way. Make sure your existing team members understand that true hospitality isn't simply reserved for guests. I introduce promising candidates to my team as they are sitting in the interview. I have even had team members come to the table and spend some time with candidates while I go do something else. It gives the candidate some time to ask questions that they may not feel comfortable asking me, and it gives me an idea how the candidate will interact with the team. That way, when they start training, they already feel like they know someone on the team and it isn't quite as uncomfortable.

- Understand what it feels like to be new someplace, and respect that. Your trainee feels disoriented, in the way, unsure, alone and incompetent. You must learn how to alleviate those feelings. Help them make friends. Elicit help from their fellow team members in facilitating their training. This will help them become comfortable with their team, and when they see that their new friends aren't going to judge or ridicule them for their lack of knowledge, but help them, they will be more at ease and there will be fewer distractions from the important information that you will impart on them.

- As a trainer, your abilities (and value) are reflected by the ongoing development, knowledge and performance demonstrated by your trainee after training.

- Adopt a system that you adhere to for each trainee. Such as; Tell, Show, Do, Review. Tell the person what you want them to do, show them how to do it, have them perform the task, then have them recap the process. Hold them accountable to the standard strictly and correct their mistakes in real time, relentlessly. There are many styles and variations that you can adopt, and no doubt your company has already outlined this for you. If not, do some research or ask for help from an experienced trainer and begin to build your own system. If you have a system that has been put in place for you, don't reinvent the wheel. Master the process and make small adjustments based on your style.

• If they make a mistake, let them know that it is alright. Do not create a culture where people fear making a mistake. Kindly correct them and have them perform the task again and make sure they understand the importance of *why* things are done that way.

• Keep up with the administrative side of things. Tests, files, e-learning, videos, whatever your system, keep up with it. Chances are your business is evaluated on how well you do this.

• Train for perfection. Set the bar high right from the get-go. Train by the book. Rigidly. People will find their own shortcuts and as long as the end result is the desirable one, that is totally fine! Spend your time fighting battles that are important, not micromanaging how Sally chooses to spec her tables. It is the end result that is important. However, it is very important that they learn the proper, systematic way to do things from the start. If they later find short cuts that don't negatively impact the P&L, the guest experience, the integrity of the brand, or the quality of the hospitality, service or product—then don't worry about it. Teach them the right way.

- Have frequent discussions with your boss about your trainees. Often, you will only have a short time to complete the training, so it is important that you communicate the person's progress. Attitude, aptitude, motivation, teamwork, organization—everything. If you have a person that you can clearly tell is not going to cut it, make that decision early before you waste more money or time or damage team morale.

- Develop and adhere to a system for validating knowledge. For example, my current training manuals have several questions at the end of each training module. At graduation, I review each question with the new team member, and ask them questions about our more popular menu items. I take notes, and I review those notes with the trainer and the department manager to make certain everyone knows what deficiencies we displayed as trainers and where the trainer and trainee did well.

- Strive for perfection and teach them to do the same. They will build this into their culture and it makes it easier for them to teach this standard to future additions to the team

- As a trainer, always be looking for ways to make your training sessions fun, look for opportunities to teach, and turn bad things into great learning experiences.

- Your role as a trainer doesn't end just because you don't have a trainee. You are essentially part of the management team. You have a responsibility to help uphold the standards consistently, all the time, training or not. Do not send the wrong message to your team by changing how you operate once the training period ends. It will only make your job, and the job of your leadership team, harder.

After training, it is important to continue to develop your team. The best way to do that is to frequently discuss measurements and results with them. Again, asking more questions than providing answers, and making sure that they have the tools needed to be successful and to grow in their position.

Continuous improvement is very important to the success of any organization. As a trainer, you are an important component in that equation.

CHAPTER NINETEEN

YOUR BOSS'S JOB

This is a pretty easy concept, but can be hard for people, especially when they have a bad boss. It is hard to want to do something to help a bad boss. There are plenty of people out there, I'm sure, who thought I was a bad boss. I have had one or two myself.

I have also seen ego get in the way of this a lot. You can really cause yourself a lot of problems if you make this a pride thing. As if somehow having been asked to complete a task is insulting, or a burden. One of the secrets of my success is that I have always been eager, willing and able to jump in and help anyone anywhere no matter what. I have never *ever* said, "that's not my job". If I see an area where help is needed then I am always the one to offer to help out. I see team members today who flat refuse to help when asked. It just baffles me when I ask someone to go help out in a department and they huff and puff and piss and moan. The same people are always the first to want a raise and are shocked when you tell them no.

Your boss's job is to provide you with the tools, training and development for you to do your job to the best of your ability. Your boss's job will seldom be to do your job. Think about it like this, if you expect your boss to do your job, then why would they need you? A secure boss who is truly interested in getting the best YOU possible, will teach you aspects of their job, and you will gradually become able to take over that role. You should eagerly seek out every opportunity to do your boss's job.

Your first priority, though, is to make your boss's job easier by becoming excellent at your job. Essentially, you want to make your boss look damn good to his or her boss by contributing at a high level.

As you become comfortable in your position, or what Ken Blanchard calls an S4 in the Situational Leadership II model, make it easy for your boss to delegate to you. Look for opportunities to take things off of your boss's plate.

At face value, this may seem a perfectly selfless approach to ass-kissing. Instead, try thinking of it in terms of your own education. The more you learn, the more valuable you are. If you are a line cook, and your direct supervisor is the KM, ask to help with some of the inventory, ordering or scheduling. If your boss knows that you are talented at this and you can free up time for him or her to focus on other important things (and help their boss), then you have just increased the ability of your boss to take on more responsibility, and now the GM is freed up to spend time on other important things (and help their boss, too), and so on. Now your business is able to handle more and more sales and you are making more and more money.

I use front line team members as examples but the same goes for you if you are a CSR, or accountant, intern, or whatever. Look at the person directly above yourself, and figure out what you can do to help them out.

Soon you are all seen as uber-productive, and as a result, uber-promotable. Even if you aren't looking for a promotion, that is okay, but it still can't hurt financially! You get good raises year after year and you become better able to provide for your family.

Obviously, the world can't be full of top performers and it's alright not to have an overload of ambition and drive. That is not me though, and since you have made it this far, I suspect it is not you either.

Don't be too eager though. Make sure you have your job locked down first. Be an expert in as many areas as you can, and be smart enough to listen to the experts in the areas you aren't. Be helpful, be thoughtful, be proactive and be productive. Boom!

CHAPTER TWENTY

SUCK IT UP: FOLLOW LOYALLY WHEN YOU GET
PASSED UP

It has been said that in order to be a great leader, you must first learn to be a great follower.

Life is tough. Sometimes, even when you try hard at something, you fail. You can choose to take this failure personally and lash out at the establishment and all within it, or you can do what professionals do and take it as a learning experience.

As you move along in your career, it is sometimes difficult to have a clear view of how much you are ready for. Some people feel they aren't quite ready for something so they don't go for it, some people feel they are more prepared than they actually are so they push too hard too fast. These two scenarios can have very negative professional outcomes. It is rare to know exactly how prepared you are for certain tasks.

If you are like me, then you don't care. I am ambitious, and I am smart. Give me a challenge and I will attack it as aggressively as possible and the outcome will be what it is. My philosophy is that if everyone waited until they were realistically ready for the next challenge, then early American settlers wouldn't have gotten very far west. There have been a lot of times in my life when I felt I was ready for the next step, that I was ready to take on the challenge in spite of my gaps in knowledge, and was shot down. It sucks, but that's life.

Do your best to know what you don't know and work your ass off, but be prepared to hear the word no. When you are faced with the situation where your boss lets you know you have been passed up for a promotion, and take it professionally. It IS okay to defend your position (behind closed doors, in private), but it is not okay to make a blubbering, emotional ass of yourself. You will undermine all that you have worked very hard for, and your boss will remember this the next time a promotion opportunity arises. Take it in stride, and ask questions like, "What would you have liked to see from me to be your choice for this role?"

It is crucially important to note that whether or not you agree with the answer is unimportant. What is important is your boss's perception of you and your performance; and, your willingness to change that perception. Chances are, if you really were that close to landing the job, you don't really have that much to work on.

Now you have to go back out on the floor and report to the person that got your job, unless the promotion involves a transfer. Either way, the team around you knows what happened and you have to face them. It will speak very highly of your leadership and professionalism to get behind the decision, congratulate the person publically and sincerely, and then break your back to make the other person successful.

This goes for any decision that you and your leadership teams make in the future. Once a decision is made, it is the responsibility of every person in the organization to make certain that the decision is successful.

People who are seen as the person who is vocal and public about their dissent are not viewed as courageous, outspoken, and opinionated. They are viewed as unprofessional, negative, and downright cancerous. In my restaurant, these kinds of people have a very short window of time to get their head right. I will usually have one very direct conversation about attitude and expectations, and that is it. I will extricate a cancerous Team Member from my team almost immediately. Maybe as I grow and develop as a leader, I will have a more productive and impactful way to deal with this situation, but as I see it, I have a responsibility to the greater good, and it is very important not to let one disgruntled individual break the morale of the entire team.

I hope you never get passed up for anything, and I hope your road to professional success is without potholes and roadblocks, but it's not likely. Especially if you come from a less fortunate background, it is difficult to learn, change, and grow. Somewhere along the road, you will make a wrong turn that will cost you a position you thought you were ready for.

Understand, your boss made it to his or her position for a reason. If you have a good boss, they will be open with you about what you need for your development and help you achieve it. If you are not ready, a good boss will tell you that too. Leaders are judged by the quality of the leaders they create. It is in your boss's best interest to develop you, just as it is in your best interest to learn everything you can from your boss. If you do get passed up, get behind the decision as quickly as possible and learn from the experience.

PART THREE

ALTITUDE

CHAPTER TWENTY-ONE

THE HOSPITALITY LADDER

I teach my Teams that there is a vast difference between service and hospitality. In fact, it is the central concept of a question that I have asked nearly every person that I've interviewed over the last fifteen years.

Both hospitality AND service are important if you want to be successful in business. As you consider the difference between service and hospitality, consider also that you have two separate groups of guests: Those you work for, and those you work with. The ones you work for are the ones at your counter or sitting at your bar or tables. The ones you work with are the people standing beside you each day—your Team of fellow Team Members and managers. It is important that you display great mechanics of service and true hospitality to both groups if you want to be successful.

136

Now, the difference is really simple. **Service** is the mechanical set of actions and abilities you must execute and display to get the job done. Taking orders accurately, refilling beverages, delivering food in a timely fashion, cleaning your establishment, doing your side-work or opening/closing duties, to name a few. I joke that it is the stuff you can train a monkey to do. It's the easy stuff, the stuff you can teach people.

Hospitality is a feeling. It is the emotion that you impart on your colleagues and customers. Hospitality often is confused with great service. Great hospitality makes you feel warm and welcome. It is the simple art of genuinely caring about those around you and letting them know it. Hospitality forgives mistakes, and takes ownership of them. Hospitality is believing that you are here to serve, and loving it. You can't teach hospitality. Some are born with it, some come to the understanding through the enlightenment of experience, but you can't teach it. You have to hire for hospitality.

Hospitality begins behind the scenes. If you have a manager that constantly berates you and focuses on all the negative things that are done, it is much harder to deliver true hospitality. I was that manager for a time and I learned a very valuable lesson. If you find yourself in that role, find your way out immediately. We discussed in chapter one that there is no neutral energy, and that is true. The people that work beside you each day deserve the same respect and admiration you give your guests. Looking at the person cooking your food, or sending back the orders, or seating tables as anything less than an irreplaceable and supremely valuable cog in the works is foolish and arrogant. Work for each other not simply with each other and delivering that hospitality to your guests gets so much easier.

In the chapter Understand the Passion, we touched on *why* people can get so passionate about their experience in your establishment. Let's discuss the *how*.

The Hospitality Ladder

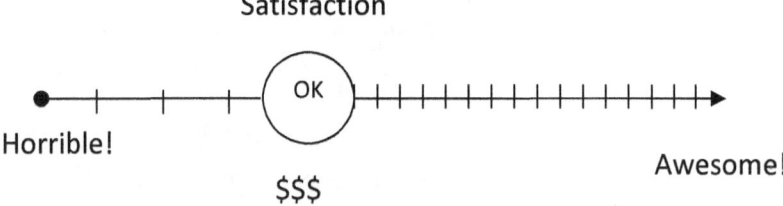

Let's work the assumption that anyone who walks through your front door begins in the middle. Each hash mark to the right and left of "OK" are rungs on the ladder that represent individual behaviors you and your team can engage in during a guest experience.

For now, they are just OK, mediocre. Maybe, since there is no truly neutral energy, they lean a little in one direction or another toward Awesome or Horrible depending on what has happened in their life that day. A person who just received a promotion is going to have a different bias than a person who just found out their grandmother died.

For all intents and purposes, whatever happened in the life of Jane Q. Guest today, we can assume that they are visiting you for a reason, and that is to have a certain experience. That experience can be as vastly unique as the stars in the sky.

I know, for example, approximately what I am going to get when I go to certain fast food chains, versus a casual dining establishment. I know about what I am going to get when I call my bank, or the cable company. I know roughly what to expect when I go to a friend's house for dinner. The variables are really up to the host in any of those situations, but I always walk in somewhere in the middle. I am "OK".

Now, the direction your guests will lean, or bias, can be greatly amplified, or completely squelched by your behavior and performance from here on out. And, you cannot just treat each person equally, it's not appropriate.

Here is how I break this down for my team:

Imagine that you walk into our restaurant. Two of your colleagues want to bring you out for lunch to celebrate your recent promotion. You like our restaurant, you eat here a few times a year, but you don't have powerful feelings either way about it. You are OK.

When you walk in, you open the door yourself and approach the host who has her back turned to you. She turns around, smiles at you and says, "Oh, hi. Sorry." She puts her phone down and asks in a pleasant enough voice, still smiling "How many?" It is clear that you have interrupted something more important to this girl than you are.

You have just taken a step to the left.

Next she rushes to a table, fifteen steps ahead of you the whole way, and drops the menus and lets you know that your server will be right over and rushes back to the host stand to pick up her text message conversation, no doubt.

The server approaches and introduces himself and asks what you would like to drink. You remember that you love our iced tea, but you like it a certain way. You have been drinking your tea like this since you were a kid, and you know precisely what you would like. As you describe it to your server, you catch the slightest hint of an eye-roll and sense of annoyance at your detailed request easily moving you one step further to the left.

Your server unceremoniously drops your tea and other beverages for the table, in a timely fashion, and whips out a pad and asks if you are ready to order. You were thinking of ordering an appetizer, but this does not seem to interest your server. No big deal, you order your entrée with sides and a side salad which you would like first. As you visit with your lunch companions, your server brings you a well timed refill, but has seemed to have forgotten how you like your tea.

Another step toward the left.

Soon your food is delivered. Your side salad did not come. The server realizes his mistake and quickly brings it out to you, and offers to take it off of your bill. Not really the point, you were looking forward to it!! Another step to the left and you have just had a horrible experience!

You are not the type to complain, so as the manager arrives at your table she phones in a quick, "how is everything?" You say fine and she goes away.

You finish your meal, leave a token fifteen percent tip—severance pay as far as you are concerned—and leave. Early in this experience you have already decided you will never be back. You get back to the office and before you clock back in, you post on every social media outlet you have access to about the horrible experience you just encountered. Your boss asks how lunch was so you tell him. Your coworkers over hear you and ask questions that you are far too happy to answer. After all, you would not want your friends and colleagues to endure what you went through!

If the manager is lucky, you will go online and submit a formal complaint to the company. If the manager is smart, she will look at this as a rare opportunity to salvage a valuable relationship. Now imagine how differently this would have all gone if the server and manager truly understood hospitality.

In guest recovery, the guest will almost always say they aren't looking for anything. People, in general, don't want to seem greedy. They do not want their complaint to be taken as a ploy to get a free meal. But they are deeply disappointed, and it is because of a broken promise. A promise that is unspoken, but implied by you to them upon their entry into your establishment. They want their disappointment to be taken seriously, and personally.

When a guest complains, what they are really saying is, "Look, I am having a horrible experience in your establishment, and you are risking losing me as a customer forever. What are you going to do about it?" How you answer that person can make or break the relationship. You want them back in your restaurant at any cost. Comp a meal for four, or never see that guest again? Think long term. I have personally taken guests from swearing they would never return and turned them into lifetime regulars in one conversation. That is a different chapter.

Nothing that happened in our first example, especially when taken as individual occurrences, was an experience-crushing event. It doesn't really matter how we think the guest _should_ feel, what matters is how the guest _actually_ feels. Owners, executives and managers, this goes for how you make your _team_ feel, too.

The point here is that, when disappointed, a guest can turn into a powerful force of destruction. Negative feedback about your business can burn through your community like an unquenchable wildfire. If you think you can afford for this to happen even one time, as a team member, manager or owner, then I am sorry to say you have a long difficult road ahead of you. Yet, how you handle that negative experience can create an equally powerful ally and friend.

Now, let's take a different look the same experience. You walk in at "OK". But as you approach the front door, it opens for you and you are greeted with good eye contact, a warm smile and a sincere "welcome!" Big step toward "awesome", right? The manager recognizes you from a previous visit and greets you with a firm hand shake and addresses you by name. Please take a step to the right. The host, beaming with energy, thanks you for coming today and asks in a professional manner how many will be joining you for lunch. She walks with you to a table, engaging you in conversation, and by doing that she discovers that you are celebrating a promotion. She gives you a sincere "Congratulations! That is awesome!"

Please take another step to the right.

She seats you and introduces herself and lets you know the name of your server is Brad, and that she is going to let him know you are here. As she walks away, you casually mention to your friends that you love a particular brand of soda that the restaurant doesn't carry. Unbeknownst to you, she takes note of that.

Your server arrives in a crisp and clean uniform and says, "Ladies, welcome! My name is Brad and I will be serving you today." He then looks you square in the eye and says "And, I understand you are celebrating today. Congratulations on your promotion! That is awesome!" Please take a step to the right. After a neatly tailored menu presentation and specific recommendations of a couple of great appetizers, you decide on an iced tea since you know they don't carry your brand of soda. Brad arrives at your table with drinks for your colleagues and an empty glass of ice for you. You are a bit confused, and maybe just a little irritated. Just as you are about to ask about this, the host that seated you arrives with a bottle of your brand of soda she bought at the grocery store next door and sets it on the table. At this point you are just blown away.

Big step to the right please.

The rest of the experience is great. Your drinks stay refilled, your food is perfect, and the server is courteous and available—but not overbearing

Step to the right.

As you finish the meal, the manager approaches your table and says "ladies, please pardon my brief interruption, my name is Tony and I am the service manager here. I want to check in before you left and make sure we are doing a great job for you today. Did we prepare everything exactly the way you like it?" Of course the answer is a resounding "YES!" He politely excuses himself, but not before addressing you by name, and congratulating you on your promotion. He even offers to buy you a dessert to help celebrate.

Big step to the right. You just landed on Awesome!

The rest of the meal finishes with much of the same attention to detail and you have already decided that this is your new favorite restaurant.

When you get back to the office, you get on social media, but this time to thank the restaurant for helping you celebrate. You tell your boss and anyone who will listen to you all day about the kind of experience you had. You brag for days and relish the opportunity to jump into discussions regarding the restaurant and share your experience. You even fill out the Guest Satisfaction Survey and write a letter to the head office bragging about Brad and his impeccable hospitality!

This is a huge win! You just created a guest for life. You should strive for this level of hospitality in whatever role you fill whether that be toward your colleagues or your guests. Always seek ways to elevate your hospitality. Don't do it to get promoted. Don't do it for yourself, and certainly don't do it for your boss. Do it with a true passion for spreading joy for the sake of others, and your rewards will be great.

Look, if you focus on the goal of Guest Satisfaction Scores, you are looking in the wrong place and you will miss not only the bigger picture, but an essential universe of details that would better help you achieve your goal.

If you are focused on the money, or your tips, then you are in it for the wrong reasons and the true nature of what it takes to realize long term (financial) success in this business will escape you.

However, if you approach your job each day with a sincere passion for making people happy and touching people's lives with the magic of hospitality, and focus on all of the rungs on the right side of The Hospitality Ladder, then you cannot fail at either goal. Your guests will be so far beyond satisfied that they will be avid fans and your greatest advocates in the community, and you will need a bigger piggy bank.

It is worth noting, that the Horrible! end of the spectrum is short and finite. It doesn't take much to ruin a guest experience. The Awesome! side is much longer, with more steps, but it is also infinite! There are so many little things you can do to build a true hospitality experience! The difference is simply doing them. Just remember how intense and personal the simple act of eating can be.

None of us work for free, and guest satisfaction and the related scores are important. Hit every rung on the right side of the ladder, the right way, for the right reasons and long term success at whatever you choose to do in life will be yours.

CHAPTER TWENTY-TWO

THE SHARK THEORY

This is another one of my cheesy metaphors that my team mocks me mercilessly for, but it works. I will admit, it is based on some flawed biological science, but it's okay. Don't over think it.

The Shark Theory relates to how you work as a manager or Team Member every day. This is not a strictly restaurant based theory, though I will frame it in restaurant terms since that is what I do for a living. You can apply this to many things restaurant or otherwise. Here it is:

If you always have your eyes open, your head on a swivel, bite (act on) the things you see, keep your hands full and your feet moving, you will never die. Never stop swimming and you will never die.

360° awareness of your surroundings is just good advice in general, but it is critical to success in any restaurant! In order to be successful in this business, you must have a razor-like awareness of every detail. I can walk into my dining room at any time of day and tell you within seconds if there is a light out somewhere. I can tell if the lights are just a little too bright. I know the condition of the restrooms. I know everything about my restaurant at all times. And it is because I spend a lot of time in the kitchen and in the dining room, restrooms and looking at the outside of my building paying attention to the smallest details. I can sense when something is out of place.

As a team member, the idea is to never waste steps. If you go to the dining room, make sure you run some food or drinks. When you come back, make sure you bring some dirty dishes. If you see trash on the floor, pick it up. If you take dirty dishes to the kitchen, bring some clean ones back with you. Never waste a step! Any step taken without something in your hands is wasted!

The most important part of your environment to be in tune with are the guests! You need to be aware of every glance, finger tap, smile or sigh. You need to see empty glasses, dirty plates and dropped napkins.

You should have a constant pattern, known as a figure 8, that you and your fellow sharks "swim" throughout the building and you should be keen to anything out of place and bite it immediately! Sharks act decisively and instinctively based on

149

keen, well sharpened instincts and being completely in tune with their environment.

Imagine working with twenty people any given day, all of whom were in tune with their environment and practicing The Shark Theory! Your establishment is packed and people just keep on coming through the door! What a great feeling to know that everyone in the building is keenly aware of their environment and taking decisive, informed action to achieve the common goal of top-flight guest hospitality! It's a pretty cool thing to be a part of.

Awareness is not enough, though. Results depend on successful execution. The gap between awareness and successful execution is very simple—decisive, informed action. Awareness without decisive, informed action is useless.

CHAPTER TWENTY-THREE

"BEN" SERVICE AND SALES BUILDING

I want to tell you about Ben.

I love, and I mean *love* to dine out. Especially as my training and knowledge increase, I really get a thrill out of dining with a team of people that truly cares about the quality of my experience, and executes it flawlessly. I have an intense eye for detail, and when people nail it, I really get charged!

Ben, unbeknownst to Ben, gave me some of the best service and treated me and a friend to some of the best hospitality I have ever experienced.

Early in the summer of 2013, I went home to Iowa to visit friends and family. On Sunday, I called my friend Elisa and asked if she'd like to go have dinner somewhere and maybe drink a little wine. We both like to sit at a bar and talk and drink and eat, so we chose a nice Italian chain restaurant nearby and agreed to meet around four that afternoon. I arrived a little early, and as I pulled into the parking lot I made a mental note of how few cars were around.

As I expected, I walked in and I was the only person, aside from Team Members, in the place. The young host greeted me unremarkably and I indicated that I would be dining at the bar.

The bartender, neatly groomed and wearing a crisply pressed white shirt, black slacks, and a black vest, made good eye contact with me and offered a welcoming smile. As he approached, he offered me a seat, which I accepted. He had a very confident and professional demeanor. After I was comfortable on my stool, he extended his hand, looked me in the eye and said "Hello. My name's Ben, what's yours?"

Wow.

"Tony," I said as I shook his hand.

"Tony, will you be dining with me today?" he asked, as he placed a cool glass of water in front of me. Again, it was Sunday. My friends know how to get down on a Saturday night in Des Moines, so this glass of cool water was just exactly what the doctor demanded. My check liver light had been flashing furiously for the last four hours.

"Yes," I said, "I am meeting a friend for wine and appetizers."

"That's great! What is your friend's name?"

I told him Elisa's name. He asked me if I would be interested in hearing the features for the day and I said absolutely. Ben proceeded to give me a brief, but tantalizing description of the culinary features that day focusing on two things, wine and appetizers. I have been in this business long enough to know that he was tailoring his spiel precisely to me based on our conversation, and he did a damn fine job! He did not get long winded, but he used descriptive flavors and profiles as he expertly paired each appetizer with an appropriate wine, letting me know that each of the wines he suggested were among his personal favorites on the list. Ben then did something rather unexpected but absolutely delightful.

He asked, "Tony, what is your favorite wine?"

"Lately I have really been into Malbec," I said.

Ben turned without saying a word. When he returned he had a small sample of red wine. "Malbecs are some of my favorite wines," he said. "Try this one, I think you will enjoy it." I thanked him and Ben excused himself and returned with a basket of warm fresh bread and prepared me a plate of cracked pepper, olive oil, and fresh grated parmesan cheese, or Italian Butter as it is sometimes called.

Keep in mind, that I am the only person at the bar. In fact, I am probably still the only person in the restaurant at this point. Ben is not intrusive, but engages me in good conversation when appropriate. We discuss wine, he asks me where I am from and we had a nice chat.

Before Elisa arrives, a couple walks in and sits at the bar. Ben welcomes them by name and gets a couple of drinks ready for them without needing to ask. Another, older, couple comes in, "Ben!" the man exclaims. "Hi there John. Cindy, good to see you, how is Jen liking her new job?"

Things continue this way for a few minutes. It reminded me of the Billy Joel song, The Piano Man except instead of nine o'clock on a Saturday, it was four thirty on a Sunday and the regular crowd was certainly shuffling in.

Ben greeted them all by name and engaged in personal conversation with each person and they all—and I mean every single one of them—responded in kind. The bar, including the tables which Ben was working as well, was filling up fast. All of the other servers who were coming in for their shifts were milling about the front door waiting for their catch.

About twenty minutes after I arrived, my friend joined me. Ben approached with a cool glass of water and set it in front of her. "You must be Elisa," he said. Elisa, as you can imagine, was duly impressed.

Ben recommended some wines to Elisa and she and I decided on some appetizers. We sat and drank and ate and chatted catching up on each other's kids and families. All the while, Ben kept getting busier and busier. Even though he had a full bar top and three or four tables, Ben never lost his cool, or even broke a sweat as far as I could tell. After we finished our food and wine, all recommendations of Ben's, we had a couple of after dinner drinks at his suggestion.

We had a great time. By the time we left, Ben was still busy, and most of the other servers were still milling around looking bored and broke.

I have had the pleasure of being attended to by masters of hospitality several times, and it is always exciting for me. I really love watching people who are truly great at what they do. It is always interesting to me to watch the habits that they have shaped and perfected over the years.

So, the great hospitality that Ben provided was impressive, greatly appreciated, and well rewarded with an excessive tip; but, what was more impressive to me was how he utilized this skill to the maximum financial benefit of himself, and his business. Ben was busy as hell when everyone else was milling around and probably bitching about being so slow. Maybe some of the others that were on duty at the time were watching and learning. Maybe not. Perhaps some wondered what his secret was, and asked him about it. Perhaps not.

What Ben does is something that is growing increasingly rare as generation after generation grows exponentially more distant from small farm town work ethic and values.

Ben understands that no one would just give him anything, at least not anything to his standards. Great rewards are earned. He appreciates and pays attention to the fine details that go into making a powerfully positive first impression. He built his own business from scratch and cultivated a client base from (possibly) years of developing firm, genuine, trusting relationships with people who love to be served by someone with such genuine concern for them. Ben didn't treat a single person at his bar like a customer. He treated them like friends. My guess is that many of them are friends.

Day to day, I watch and coach people who greet people with a demand for an order. "Hi. Something to drink?"

Are you asking me? Or, telling me? This is not a good sales technique, nor is it good hospitality. Whether you are a leader, a sales person, or a producer, then you will be well served by the knowledge that each day you are responsible for creating and nurturing relationships.

Today in fact, I walked into a reputable chain coffee shop and the first thing that anyone said to me was what can I get started for you.

What about "hello"? What about "how are you today"? How about a "thanks for coming in"?

Nope, just business. That is why this stop is a stop of convenience, not an emotional necessity. For me, and many other people, I spend my ten to fifteen hour long days caring for other people and I really enjoy (and reward) when I receive the same in return.

The thing is, it's really not that hard. It is as simple as the understanding that it isn't about you. Whether you are a parent, teacher, barista, manager, server, janitor, cook or President of the United States, then you are part of a system that thrives when we serve one another and treat each other with respect and mutual interest—without expecting anything in return.

Ben knows where his money comes from. Yet, in the two hours that we sat at his bar, not one time did he ever count his tips or even look at a credit card receipt. He was focused on the guest. Ben understood that his small business would thrive as long as he focused on the right thing--people, and he is a true master of it.

The company that Ben worked for would be foolish not to recognize his value. I absolutely guarantee that if Ben were to accept a position at a Mexican restaurant across the street or even across town, that many of the patrons I shared my Sunday with would change their Sunday routine and visit him wherever he chose to set up shop.

Sales building is everyone in the organization's responsibility. No matter what role you play, the quality of your work is vitally important to the success of the business. So, play your part well. Sometimes it is easy to see how, for example the role a cook might play in the sale growth of a restaurant. It might not be as easy to see how you play a role if you are far removed from the front lines, like an accountant.

If a cook puts out great food consistently and takes pride in the product he allows the clientele to receive, then it is likely the restaurant will be successful, and sales will increase. If the cook doesn't care and is happy to punch a clock and get his check without concern for the quality of his product, it will be much more challenging for the business to succeed. Cook sends out bad food, servers get stressed, bad food and stressed server snowballs into bad hospitality and service and that leads to a guest who will not likely return and then tells two hundred Facebook friends of their experience. Soon, you are wondering why you are looking for work.

It really doesn't take much extrapolation to see how one person's poor performance can have a huge negative impact on the overall business. As an accountant, it may be hard to see how your performance impacts the overall operation, but everything snowballs into something else.

Once, I worked with a payroll specialist who was just terrible at her job. She was disorganized and frequently I had issues that I had to deal with relating to her and her department. She would lose documents, and I would have to resubmit them. I literally spent hour upon valuable hour each week chasing her shortcomings. What is the opportunity cost of that lost time? It's hard to quantify, but it is a significant loss and distraction I can tell you.

Now, on the contrary, let's say you have an excellent team focused on tremendous hospitality and excellent products and service. As a cook and a professional, you are committed to self-improvement and self-education and you know the food better than anyone else in the company. You believe that serving excellent food that looks and tastes great is not only your passion, but your duty. Your plates not only look great, they are produced quickly and accurately, mistakes for you are rare. You feel great pride and enjoyment from seeing guests faces light up when your plates are served.

As a result, the service team is able to focus on the level of hospitality they provide and people rave about your establishment every chance they get. Sales are through the roof and you receive frequent raises and rewards. Soon, you are asked to take the responsibility of training new Team Members. A few months later you are promoted to an hourly manager position. You are so successful at training new people and creating a culture of excellence in sales and profits, that you are asked to be the new

Kitchen Manager at the new location that your boss has decided to open—thanks, in part, to your commitment to excellence.

As you prove your value to the organization, your career will progress and your wealth will increase. That is just the way it works. Remember, luck is the intersection between hard work, opportunity, positive attitude and good decision making.

Ben increases his value each and every day, and whether or not it is deliberate, the impact he makes reflects on his restaurant's profit and loss statement each week. Which direction do you think Ben's life and career are headed?

CHAPTER TWENTY-FOUR

NO MAN'S LAND: LEADING WITHOUT A TITLE

This one chapter is probably my fundamental inspiration for writing this book. Personally, I really struggled with this concept. Professionally, I have seen it cripple dozens of people who just could not get past the idea of leading without a title.

Recently, I had a very talented cook who chose to be devastatingly negative. I worked and worked with him to be more positive and to try to have a positive impact on the people around him. I truly believed that if he could get to a positive place that he would be a truly great KM. He was a natural leader, and people followed him. Unfortunately, utilizing his charisma and leadership, he was able to spin up so much negativity that he crippled our kitchen. At the end of the day, he chose not to remove his roadblocks, and after many open and honest conversations, we could not help him. In spite of his skill and talents, we made the difficult decision to fire him. Morale immediately improved—in spite of the loss of his significant productivity and skill that the team suffered.

Lead without a title? Take on responsibility before I am paid to do so? What are these words you say? Yeah, it's possible to have an impact even without the gold nametag. In fact, you probably won't be able to get your gold nametag until you prove yourself first, and guess what--that includes leading people, proving your ability to hold yourself and others accountable, and taking on more responsibilities. You can argue whatever you want against it, and good luck in your career. I am here to tell you, be the person that makes your boss's job easier, takes on more responsibility, and creates a positive impact on the business in as many ways possible, and you will be on the short list of people to get promoted.

This chapter will be short and sweet and most of it is as simple and bulleting a few lessons that I learned over the years that I hope help you:

- Titles come because of leadership, not before it.

- Power is not a leadership attribute, it's a responsibility bestowed upon people who know how to lead.

- Leadership is a personal attribute, not a title.

- If you can't lead without a title, then you won't lead with one.

- People do not follow the title, they follow the person.

- Natural leaders (charisma) will lead people which ever direction they choose to go, and that is not always good. Check your attitude.

- Leadership can be learned and developed.

- Leadership is more about other people than it is about you.

- Leaders create, nurture and develop; never destroy, damage or stagnate.

- Leaders understand that they are human and therefore imperfect, and so are others.

- Leaders lead through integrity, trust and by setting the example.

- Leaders never say things like, "I'm here to work, not here to make friends"…life is a lot easier when you spend it with people you like, and positive relationships are crucial to your success.

That is a good start. Wrap your head around these ideas, and you will be on a pretty good path toward developing yourself as a leader. Do not get too wrapped up in the *how*, just do it. Do not over complicate things and don't over think it. It is not as mysterious as it sounds. Be a positive and impactful person and be nice to people, and you will be fine.

CHAPTER TWENTY-FIVE

THE MYSTERIES OF THE P&L

Having trained dozens of people to take leadership roles from hourly positions, I have heard one fear expressed more than any other, "But I don't understand the P&L". This will be a very short chapter.

I can tell you all you really need to know, as a new manager, about the P&L in one sentence:

Don't worry about it.

That's right. Don't spend a lot of time wringing your hands for fear that you won't understand the numbers. Don't get me wrong, when you see a Profit and Loss statement (essentially your restaurants report card), or transaction register, or cost detail, or labor detail report for the first time it can be overwhelming and intimidating. But relax, the numbers are the easiest part of the job.

All the numbers really do is report to you how you are doing with the people. If you have the right people and you are managing your team effectively, the numbers will take care of themselves. You just need to learn to read them, and once you do, you will feel a bit silly for being so worked up. Any good teacher could sit down and teach you what all of those lines of data translate to, and where the information comes from in about an hour. From there it is practice.

You as a manager or owner will be responsible for what those numbers say. In any restaurant, your two most expensive things are Food, and Labor. Those two categories alone can consume 50% or more of your sales in a pretty big hurry if you don't manage things effectively. So, what does that tell you? You should probably spend a lot of time with your food, and with your team and not so much with your reports.

Again, you definitely need a basic understanding of math. You need to learn where the numbers come from and how your reports pull data. You need to understand addition, subtraction, multiplication, division, and how percentages are calculated. But, you don't need to be a math genius at all.

Now on the P&L, there are a few numbers that are of key importance to you as a manager. Different companies may use different terminology for each category, although many are similar if not the same. I picked the most common ones that I have worked with and I will give you a brief description of them here:

Top Line Sales—This is how much revenue (money) your business generated for the selected timeframe (day, week, month, quarter, or year). This is the Top Line of the P&L, hence the name, but this can also be called Gross Sales.

BWL Cost—This is the cost of your bar sales. Each line will likely be broken out separately, and the dollar cost will be divided by the dollar sales to get your percentage.

Food Cost—This is how much the food you sold cost your restaurant. This is the dollar cost of the food divided by the dollar amount of sales. The formula for this is Beginning Inventory+Purchases-Ending Inventory=Usage/Food Sales.

COGS—Cost of Goods Sold. This is the combined total cost of all of the food and beverage that you sold, a.k.a. Cost of Sales.

Gross Profit—This is your profit less discounts, and cost of sales.

Labor—This is what your hourly labor cost your restaurant.

Total Payroll—This includes everything from the labor category, and also payroll taxes, insurance, and management salaries.

Controllable Expenses—There can be many lines under this category and they are called "Controllable" for a reason.

167

Profit After Controllable Expenses—This is the money you get to look at just before you pay rent, etc. Also known as EBITDA or EBITDAR at my current company

Non-Controllable Expenses—This includes rent, depreciation and other expenses that you usually cannot impact through day to day management. Also called Fixed Expenses.

Net Profit—This is how much money your business contributes to the company, or owner. A good rule of thumb, though this can be vastly different depending on your business model, is that this number should be greater than 10%. This is known as "the bottom line".

Having a good understanding of these numbers and where they come from is not complicated. Each company will have various methods for reporting, but there won't be drastic differences in the data or where it comes from. The reason it is important to understand where this information comes from, is so that you can verify the accuracy of the reports. It isn't hard for someone to make a clerical error that can skew your numbers. It is crucial to make certain that these numbers are accurately reported to your superiors. Remember, manage your numbers. Lead your people.

CHAPTER TWENTY-SIX

SOME NOTES ON COST CONTROL

Different places manage cost in different ways, but most places with good POS Systems and inventory management systems use what is called a Theoretical Variance to manage their inventory management performance. That is, they manage the gap between what they *should have* used versus what they *actually* used.

Other companies use a straight percentage as a guideline to manage food cost. This method can be deceptive, since you do not always sell the same combination of things week to week. This combination of products sold is known as your Product Mix, P Mix, or Sales Mix. The Theoretical Variance really allows you to be more detailed because it is based on a theoretical usage which comes from the food and beverage you actually sold. If you go on a straight percentage, you could be hitting your numbers, yet wasting a lot of food, and essentially leaving money on the table.

The foundation of maintaining excellent food cost is reporting inventory accurately. The three pillars of reporting accurate inventory are proper ordering, proper receiving, and proper organization.

Proper ordering of all products is vital. Only order what you need to get by until your next order. Ideally, you should be pulling the last of something from the shelf as the truck backs up to the door. This is called Just In Time ordering or (JIT).

To order accurately, you must manage your par levels carefully. "Par Level" refers to the minimum level of product you need in-house to satisfy demand. If you are running out of something frequently, then you need to increase your pars. Build your pars from *actual* usage, NOT *theoretical*.

Manage the gap between the two by educating and coaching your Team, then reduce your pars accordingly as you get better at execution. Yes it is true that you can't waste it if you don't have it, but you also can't give it to your guests. To me, there is no bigger waste of time and other resources than having to go pick something up from someplace that sends you a truck twice a week. And, if you take the approach of "when we're out, we're out", then you aren't sending a very good message to your team or your guests, and you are missing out on sales by providing poor hospitality. Don't be stubborn, and manage the right things and you'll be alright.

Below is a sample of how you might set a par level using a spreadsheet as an order guide. Each week, you can see there is an On Hand quantity (OH), an Order quantity (OR), and a Usage (U). Your formula for calculating the Usage for Week 1 is the OH + OR – W2 OH = W1 U. So, 1 + 3 – 1 = 3. You used 3 of Product 1 in Week 1, 4 in Week 2 and so on. You take your total usage and divide it over the number of weeks of data you have collected and you come up with your average weekly usage. You come up with 3.25 for your Par level. When placing your order, you know that if you have 3.25 or less, then you need to order it. Practice for yourself by setting the Par Level for Product 3.

A	B	Week 1			Week 2			Week 3			Week 4			Week 5		
Item	PAR	OH	OR	U	OH	OR	U	OH	OR	U	OH	OR	U	OH	OR	U
Product 1	3.25	1	3	3	1	3	4	0	4	3	1	3	3	1		
Product 2	5	4	1	5	0	4	4	0	5	5	0	7	6	1		
Product 3		0	2		1	0		0.5	1		0	2		1		

Now, you can argue effectively that since you spiked to a usage of 4 in Week 2 that you want to set your Par Level to 4. That's fine. Pay attention to the shelf life of the product and be certain you aren't jeopardizing health, or quality. You and your boss may decide that you want to build a cushion into your par levels. That's totally fine too. Again make sure you are not getting carried away. The fewer products you have in house, the less you can lose or waste.

The goal is to have as little product on the shelves as possible and not lose any sales due to out of stock items. You can run things pretty tight and still have zero out of stocks. When you first begin dialing things in, you may run out frequently. It is okay to build your cushion a little heavy at first and dial things back, rather than starting too thin and trying to catch up. Doing it this way creates fewer opportunities for you to have to explain to a guest why you are out of something and therefore less stress for you, your team and for your boss. Even more important, you can't sell it if you don't have it. If your guests cannot count on you to have their favorite items in stock, they will go somewhere else. It does not take long for that decision to be made either. It won't take very many times letting your guests down for that decision to become permanent. Make sure you stay on top of it and make needed adjustments quickly.

Proper receiving of the product you ordered is vital. You are paying for it, doesn't it make sense to take the time and ensure that you are receiving what you paid for? Check for four things (PQQP):

1. Product—Is it there and is it the right thing. Boxes get mislabeled and mispicked all the time, so check thoroughly.

2. Quality—Don't accept it if you can't use it. Purveyors are insured for this kind of thing. Don't feel bad for sending something back.

3. Quantity—If you receive something by an "each" unit of measure, then make sure you got the right quantity. If it is received by a "weight" unit of measure, then throw it on a scale and weigh it.

4. Price—Are you paying what you are supposed to pay for this product. Don't take this for granted. Know what you are supposed to pay and double check. There are too many humans involved in the process and mistakes happen all the time.

Proper organization in your restaurant is vital. Everything should be organized using the FIFO (First In, First Out) system and everyone on your team should know how this works. There should be a labeled place for every item you inventory, and each shift you should verify that everything has been put back in its labeled place.

Now, you know you have ordered properly, you know your kitchen is organized and clean, and you know that you received everything exactly right, and you know your inventory is 100% correct. So it stands to reason that your food cost is perfect now, right? Wrong. What you have done is created a stable foundation on which you can firmly stand as you manage your team. You still need to coach them and teach them and hold them accountable to specs and standards. You still have to check portion sizes and best practices. But now you know you aren't going to jump down someone's throat for losing twelve pounds of tomatoes that you never received or that you miscounted!

Now, when managing your people and your food, remember that you can only lose food in five places. Plate, Trash, Mouth, Trunk, and Air. Wasted food can go on to a guest's **plate** as over portioning or as a result of a cook giving the server something without it being rung in. Things can also go in the **trash** as waste due to misuse (remember that accident, carelessness and neglect are all very similar) or over-prepping, into someone's **mouth** as an unpaid for snack (theft), into someone's **trunk** (theft), and it can literally vanish into thin **air** through evaporation by cooking down or being held for too long on the line.

Food cost can be very tricky to manage, but it is a lot of fun once you get your team on board and see them take ownership of the numbers and put up good results. Share all of this information with your team as frequently as possible.

If you are responsible for ordering other items for your business, like paper goods for example, you will have a budget you must follow in order to be a financially successful business. A lot of places use what is called a Declining Budget to manage this. Something that has been very successful for me has been what I call (with tongue in cheek and a nod to the declining budget) a "REclining Budget".

A Declining Budget uses your forecasted sales as a basis for ordering products based on what your business's budget allows for. For example, if you are allowed to spend a total of .01% of your sales on paper supplies and your forecasted sales are $180,000.00 for the upcoming period, then you would be able to spend $180.00 that month on paper. This method works pretty well. My only issue with the Declining Budget is that you rarely ever hit your projections exactly so then you end up playing guessing games month to month. I have modified it to take much of the guess work out of the process.

My modification, the "Reclining Budget", is different in the sense that I am looking backward rather than forward. On the first Monday of the month, I order exactly .01% of my previous month's sales, or less. On my controllable expense lines, I am always perfect at the end of the year. There will be times when you have special events or holidays coming up that you will have to make adjustments for, but that is easy. If I overdo it, then I just make adjustments the following month, applying the difference to my next order.

As you learn the ins and outs of the P&L, it is important that you learn to manage each line effectively. Setting proper pars, managing usage, engaging in highly accurate ordering practices and procedures, and knowing your budget will set you up so that you almost have to try to fail. The rest is a combination of knowledge, participation, training, execution, and simply paying attention.

CHAPTER TWENTY-SEVEN

DEALING WITH THEFT

I get asked how to deal with this a lot. There aren't many things that aggravate me more than a thief. And, unfortunately it is just part of the job that you will have to deal with from time to time. Rule number one: Never, **ever** accuse someone of theft unless you have undeniable proof. If you make the wrong accusation, then you can severely damage an otherwise good relationship.

If you have undeniable proof, terminate the person immediately with another manager present. If you catch them red handed and you are the only one around, send them home and let them know they need to speak with you and your GM before their next scheduled shift. Chances are, they aren't coming back, but if they do then you are not having the confrontation alone.

If you are doing the right things, you will make it very hard for people to steal from you. First hire the right people. If you hire someone and all of the sudden you start missing things, it's a good bet you know who to watch. As they feel the pressure of you watching, they will be much less likely to steal.

If you are where you should be, and that is not in the office checking social media, then it will be hard for anyone to steal.

If you create a fun work environment where people feel well rewarded and respected, they will be much less likely to want to steal.

If you keep your high value items locked up then they will be less able to steal.

If you do suspect someone of theft, then let that person see you frequently counting and verifying inventory of the missing items. Check your inventory before and after their shifts. If something comes up missing, but you cannot prove it is them who stole it, you can still talk to them, but be careful of your tone. You might say, "hey John we came up missing a bottle of bourbon last night, did you see anyone behind the bar that wasn't supposed to be there?" John will likely say no, and that is really it. John knows your watching. If it happens again, then you have another conversation to have, and you also have an emerging pattern.

"John this is the second time a bottle of liquor has come up missing on your shift. As the bartender, you are responsible for maintaining an accurate inventory back there. Do you have any ideas where we are losing this?"

You aren't throwing accusations, but you are holding John accountable. Who knows, maybe there is a legitimate reason for the shortage. Wouldn't you feel foolish if you accused someone of stealing and then a legitimate reason surfaced? Still, use common sense. If you are missing something there are only a few places it can be and if your bartender is losing a bottle of bourbon regularly on his shift, that is a problem no matter how you slice it. If he is over-pouring that heavily or not paying attention while someone else is stealing, then that is a problem too.

Hire good people, lead them well, manage your business, make it fun to come to work, take away temptation, and act swiftly and decisively if you do catch a thief. That's really all you can do.

CHAPTER TWENTY-EIGHT

CREATING THE MATRIX: STAYING COMPLIANT

If you work in a privately-owned or corporate environment, or even if you have your own small business, there are going to be tons of things that you have to keep up with. Things that you are going to have to make sure that you and everyone on your staff completes. Maybe that is wine training, or getting a signature on a specific form, but whatever it is, you need to make sure that everyone gets it done.

It's pretty simple to keep track of these things, really. I have always used what I call a compliance matrix and I check it each week to ensure that I am 100% up to date with all team member requirements. You can use it for regularly occurring inspections, forms, or really anything you need to make sure that multiple people get done.

What I do is create a simple Excel spreadsheet with the far left column being a list of my team member's names. Each column will be labeled with a different required test or document, or group such as "E-Learning". For grouping things like E-Learning for example, I don't necessarily track each person's progress except to verify that it is all done. When they are 100%, I check them off. It's that simple. Your goal is obviously to be 100% compliant and up to date at all times.

If you are always ahead, you are never behind. See below for a real world example. I have used variations of this for years.

	A	B	C	D	E	F	G	H	I
1	Compliance Matrix	FILE			MSDS BINDER	HAZZ COMM			E-Learning
2		Present?	Audit Sheet?	Tests?	Signed?	Present?	Complete?	Courses %	Test %
3	Employee 1								
4	Employee 2								
5	Employee 3								
6	Employee 4								
7									

I usually have a copy printed on a clipboard where it is easily seen by all team members. Then I simply follow up with all non-compliant team members on my shifts and keep pushing them to get these things done, and check them off once I personally visually verify their completion. Keeping careful track of these types of things really makes your job so much easier. If you don't keep up with this stuff, your boss has to do it and it is a big waste of time for them and a pretty big black mark for you.

Even once you have everything completed and you haven't hired any new team members for a while, it is a good idea to recheck your team's files once a quarter or so. It's easy in a busy work environment for pieces of paper to get lost or misfiled. You don't want to be the one telling your boss you are 100% on something and then get dinged for it on an inspection. That never looks or feels very good.

The cool thing about Excel, is that you can just keep adding to the sheet as your boss adds to your pile of duties. This method is simple, neat, tidy and super easy to keep up with.

CHAPTER TWENTY-NINE

FRATERNIZATION

Well you are on your way. Congratulations. You are up for promotion and you are now facing the challenge of being responsible for the performance of the same people that you have worked beside and probably had one or two dozen beers with. What should you do?

First of all, it is generally bad practice to sleep with anyone you work with. It never ends as fun as it starts and there is always way too much drama surrounding the aftermath. So, scratch that. But can you manage your friends effectively?

The company that you work for will undoubtedly have an opinion on this, and as a professional who buys in to the company mission and values, you should honor that opinion. Companies lay out blanket policies relating to fraternization for two reasons.

One, it is difficult to apply different standards to different people and avoid legal and ethical complications. Two, it is easy for you to make a terrible mistake while hanging out with subordinates thereby causing legal complications. Larger corporations especially have some stronger opinions on this. There are real and valid concerns here that you would be wise to respect.

I have managed many, many of my friends and family members quite successfully. I can't say I was exceptionally careful about my behavior when we were hanging out either. We all did lot's of shots, broke lot's of rules and had a hell of a good time. We worked hard, and played hard and made lots of money. But, when we worked, we understood the relationship. I had a meeting when I got promoted and I let the team know what they could expect from me, and very, very rarely did I ever have to have another conversation about performance. But we worked for a small company, and I knew all of my team very well.

If your company is bigger, and they are that worried about it, they will move you to a different location. If they don't, then you need to be very careful about perceived favoritism, harassment, and liability concerns. It is not at all unheard of for a boss to take a team member out and that person gets a DUI or has an accident and the company gets sued. At this point, go ahead and polish up your résumé.

It is unlikely any of you are going to scrap years-long relationships due to a promotion. Treat everyone equally and be smart, and don't flaunt it to your boss. Definitely don't engage in any illegal or unethical behavior with anyone that works for you, and don't put yourself (or your company) in the position to take the blame for any unfortunate turns of events.

Back in the day, it was no big deal. That's just the way it was done. A GM that I worked for used to have the best parties at his house! We smoked in the office, dated the servers, drank beer after work, and it was—well, it was really great! But things have changed. In my opinion, it's unfortunate. I think that having the opportunity to have a few beers with your boss is a pretty cool reward for some people, and if we are really building relationships with people, then we need to be seen as human.

At some point in your career, you may develop feelings for someone you work with, either platonic or romantic. The heart wants what the heart wants. If a romance or close friendship develops, and one of the two of you is subordinate to the other, then the smart thing to do is to come clean to your boss. Chances are one of you will be transferred. Trust me, you don't want to be on the wrong side of the conversation if you try to hide it.

Be professional and be respectful of your company's code of conduct and you will be fine. As with anything, if you choose to go all "Broken Arrow" on the system, be prepared for the consequences. Refer back to the chapter where we discussed luck and good decision making. Making the wrong decision here can get you labeled as irresponsible and untrustworthy very quickly, and therefore derail your planned success.

CHAPTER THIRTY

CONGRATULATIONS! YOU ASKED FOR IT.

Well, kiddo, you made it. All of your hard work and dedication to making better decisions about your life has paid off. You are promoted. You just got your first entry level management position. Now what?

First, let me give you a heads up:

- You are going to make mistakes.

- There will be several points in the next six months where you wonder what the hell you were thinking by even *wanting*, much less accepting such a position. This is a highly stressful job, but there are many things you can do to reduce the level of anxiety in your day to day life. These almost exclusively deal with organization, preparedness, accountability and consistency.

187

- You are going to have a "first shift" that falls completely apart and it will be mostly your fault. We call it "Going Sideways". The good news is that if you learn (a lot) from that shift, it makes the second one much easier to manage. (Hint: the bad news is that there will be a second one too!)

- You are going to have your leadership and decisions tested and challenged every day by people who should be on your side. Figure out who those people are, and get them on your side.

- You will come on too strong sometimes and not strong enough other times. It is important to find a balance.

- You will likely be confused, overwhelmed, excited and nervous—for a while.

- Somewhere around the six-month-mark, it will all start to gel and make sense. Hang in there.

- You are going to have a strong desire to fire somebody on the spot for something at some point—don't do it.

You may have to fire someone immediately some day, but try to send them home and do it later. The message will be sent and you allow them to retain their dignity. There may arise a time that it is appropriate and necessary to end someone's employment immediately. Though, this should be the last club in your bag. There are certain benefits and HUGE detriments to using this club. On one hand, it can send a message to your team that you are the boss and you refuse to accept certain behaviors. On the other hand, it can make you look like a jerk and a bully, scare other people that work for you, and damage trust. Neither hand is great.

There have been a handful of times in my career where I have terminated people right on the spot. Some were absolutely crucial, and some were an angry response when I was early in my career.

The first time I fired someone was six months into my first management job. I had a server who was just a nightmare to manage. If I had been more experienced, maybe there were ways I could have better preserved the relationship or helped this girl be more of a team player. We will call her Amber.

We were in the middle of a crazy-busy night. As was normal, everything was going wrong for Amber and she was throwing an almighty fit. She was snapping at everyone, throwing things and breaking stuff. It was bad.

I pulled her aside and said, "Amber, I need you to calm down." Lesson number one; if you only remember one thing from this book, remember the relationship stuff. But, if you remember *two* things from this book, also remember to never tell a raging maniac who is frothing at the mouth to "calm down".

Her response was less than professional and in front of the entire team she started screaming at me and told me what I should go do to myself—it wasn't give myself a pedicure. At that time, I would have rather been doing what she suggested, believe me

My response was, "Give me your cash out and go clock out. You're fired."

She was shocked. So was everyone else. Her exact response was, "You can't fire me!" I said something terribly clever about my nametag being gold and hers being white and yes I could.

Not very professional. If I had taken that approach when I first walked in the door as a new manager, I would have alienated everyone. Could I have sent her home and talked to her later? Yes, though I doubt it would have worked. Was I seeing red and act from a place of emotion as a new and inexperienced manager? Yes. The end result was that the team appreciated that I would rather run short handed than allow the rest of them to endure her shenanigans any longer and they rallied around me. If I had not had strong relationships with the rest of them, it could just as easily have backfired on me. They could have rallied against me, and you don't want that.

Two other instances come to mind, both times were after taking over the same new restaurant team. The restaurant had been undermanaged and understaffed for a while. When I first arrived, I spent about two weeks getting to know the team, and the situation was pretty bleak. The hourly team had taken charge and they were really not very good at it. In my twenty-five years in the restaurant business and my fifteen years of management, I have never seen anything even remotely as bad.

After two weeks of getting to know the team and the situation, I made a conscious decision to exert my authority at the first strategic opportunity. By my calculation, a little fear would at least stem the tide of aggression I was receiving from all directions. Until a situation presented itself, I just continued to work with people as best I could and coached and taught the few people who would listen.

It didn't take long. Dishes were piling up on a relatively busy night and I asked one of the worst guys in the kitchen, we'll call him David, to help me catch up the dish area. I said, "David, can you please jump back in dish and help us out back there for a minute?" He said, "fuck you, it's not my job." I asked, "so, I have asked you politely for your help and that is how you respond to me?" He said, "Yep", and started to walk away. So I let him go. I said, "In that case, you can clock out. I don't need you working for me."

He gave me the bird, and left. I put another manager in charge of the floor and put on an apron and jumped on dishes and knocked out the immense pile in about thirty minutes. I then went back to the line and worked David's position for the rest of the shift. I didn't say a word about it to anyone. Soon, someone asked where David was. I told them simply that he no longer worked with us, and continued working.

My actions had three impacts, one negative and two positive. One, I sent a message to the team that I am capable and willing to do the work I am asking them to do. Two, I sent the message that I expect them to do it and if you don't want to play on my team then you don't have to. And three, I sent a message that it was my way or the highway. The last part was an unpleasant necessity in my mind. I really want to be seen as a fun guy to work for, and nobody likes working for the guy that will just can you at the first sign of trouble, but I woke the team up and grabbed their attention.

The next week I spent a lot of time attempting to repair some of that damage. I sat down with individuals one-on-one and asked them how they felt about it. I asked them what their ideas were as far as improvement. At the end of the day, what I had on my hands was about three years of very poor management and hiring decisions to correct. It took me two years to build a team of good people and strong performers and my turnover was astronomical as the mass of cancerous team members chased away any potential high quality players. We had a great team at the end of it. When you have a team of good hearted people who were raised to care about others and with good work ethic, you really begin to see a team emerge.

It can be scary once you find yourself in charge for the first time. You spend a lot of time striving for the goal, and yet you possibly haven't given a whole lot of thought to what it actually might be like. It is intense and very fast paced and there is no purer joy in the world that being the captain of a fast ship that is running full speed. Conversely, there aren't many more crushing feelings than being the captain of that same ship and taking heavy fire from all sides.

The kitchen is crashing, the front door is crashing, the floor is crashing, your dish guy just walked out and your bartender is having an emotional breakdown. Meanwhile you are visiting tables and getting very honest, real-time feedback about how each guest feels about your performance. When things are going wrong in a restaurant, each person at every table has a strong feeling they could do your job better than you, and they do not mind telling you about it. All the while, you must maintain composure and get everything back on track. It's going to happen. If you are smart, and can pay attention to more than two or three things at a time, then you will analyze what happened and fix it. After that it should happen pretty infrequently, but it *will* happen to you at some point. Do not be discouraged, and do not let your team see you sweat. They are watching you to see how you handle yourself and they will follow your lead.

As a new manager, you need to take the first six months and get acclimated to your surroundings. Get to know your people. Become a master of your surroundings. Spend time anticipating problems and fixing them before they become a reactive situation.

You will have other responsibilities like inventory, ordering and other administrative duties, but in the first six months, don't try to take on too much. You will have enough on your plate. After six months start branching out and taking on more responsibility. Take something new off of your boss's plate every week, or every month. Be a sponge and learn everything that you can about his job.

Your number one priority will always be your team and being the leader that inspires them to create great hospitality for your guests, and produce an *exceptional* product. Be a master of hospitality. The other stuff is really pretty easy.

Once you get your position, you need to understand one very important thing. You and you alone are responsible for the performance of your department. Take that responsibility seriously, and be aggressive in achieving results. The people that report to you represent you and your leadership ability. If they fail, look first at yourself and then spend ample time developing them. Get to know what makes them tick, and what motivates them. Ask more questions than you provide answers and hold them accountable to their results.

I have had managers work for me that think they are very good at their jobs. Many are incapable of setting and achieving goals, accomplishing tasks, holding people accountable, they don't spend any measureable quality time with their teams and fail to produce results. It's shocking to me to see their salaries sometimes.

Trust me. If you master the professional traits in this book, you will absolutely destroy your competition when it comes to the job market. The key is that you have to demonstrate the ability. Demonstrated ability is measured by the results you achieve. Results are accomplished through discipline and relationships. Keep a log of all of your achievements and every dime you make or save the company and discuss these things with your boss as often as you get the chance.

PART FOUR

FORTITUDE

CHAPTER THIRTY-ONE

YOUR SALARY

This is short and sweet. When you are hired or promoted as a manager, companies have a predetermined idea of what that is worth to them. Most are willing to reach above that for the right candidate. This can be a delicate situation. There are tons of resources available to you online and in bookstores on how to do this. Use them. Glassdoor.com is a very good resource full of information from people who currently work for organizations that have shared their earnings with the public at large.

As a PFW (promote from within) manager, chances are you will be offered the low end of the spectrum. This is just how it goes. Some companies will really take advantage of this though, so be careful. You should educate yourself on the industry and be knowledgeable going into the negotiation. As a PFW, you do not have a lot of negotiating power, so be cautious. From the company's perspective you are inexperienced and the experience you will receive is very valuable and you should respect that. Your inexperience can be quite costly to the company and you should respect that too. As your experience grows, and you prove yourself worthy through exceptional results, your negotiating power greatly increases. It is okay to accept the lower offer, and negotiate for a better salary as you become more experienced. When you accept the position and the salary, you might say something like this:

"I understand that my lack of experience and unproven track record in this position are the reason I am being offered this salary. The industry standard for this position is a little higher though. Would you be willing to evaluate my performance and this salary offer in six months or a year with the expectation that I could reach X dollars per year based on my performance?"

Be armed with good information and the knowledge that it is in the company's best interest to pay you fairly for your level of experience, and your service. Loyalty is a very valuable commodity, but if your company is unwilling or unable to pay you fairly, consider looking elsewhere. Be cautious not to position yourself as a person who just jumps to the next highest paycheck, as this can be professionally damaging, but you must protect yourself, your family and your financial situation first and foremost.

As a manager being hired into a new company, do your homework. Know what you are worth and be willing to walk away if you are not able to reach an agreement. Make sure you consider all factors such as culture, growth potential, and market before you act; and do not act rashly or unprofessionally.

When you negotiate, do so confidently and avoid saying things like, "it's ok if you can't do it". State your needs, and reasons why you are worth it and do so confidently. Leave it up to them to decide what they do with it. Typically, they will counter offer and you will end up somewhere between their number and yours. If you are going to play this game though, you'd better have more than one iron in the fire. A company that feels they will not be able to meet your financial needs, or feels you are being greedy will often times sever the relationship to protect the long term success of the company and your long term happiness. It does not behoove anyone for a company to bring on someone that they know will not be happy with their earnings long term.

CHAPTER THIRTY-TWO

RECRUITING, INTERVIEWING, AND HIRING

Recruiting great talent is the best way to build your business. I only have one personal rule; I don't recruit from other owners or managers who are close friends. Whether you do or not is entirely up to you. Other than that it is game on. I have personally gutted other restaurant teams taking advantage of their talent development—and their poor management practices. That may sound ruthless, but so be it. I am running a business. If I treat my team poorly, they will leave me for someone who won't. I don't see any reason why I shouldn't be the guy people want to work for.

Go out and find the best people you know and hire them. Go to popular restaurants and bars and recruit people that you know will make you successful. Recruit people who are always positive and represent their brand well. Be careful, though, I have been asked to leave places for recruiting too aggressively, and another manager in my company was recently banned for life from a local pizza joint for attempting to recruit their team and talking poorly about the owner.

You should always have a stash of business cards with you and hand them out. I have an approach that I have used successfully so that I don't look like a merciless scalper—even though that might be my intent. I hand them a card and say, "I am hiring for my restaurant. I think you would be an amazing addition to my team. If you are ever interested in a second job, I'd love to talk to you." Or, "I am hiring for my restaurant. Do you have any friends looking for work?" As I build that relationship, I may become bolder and ask directly when they are coming to work for me. Protect your investment and hire the best.

Another thing to be cautious of when you are pulling people from the same place, is that people run in packs. If you recruit someone and then they start pulling their friends over, make damn sure you have the right group of friends. It can turn sour pretty quickly if you aren't discerning. If you get a core group from one place, get them trained, and then they all leave you in six months for the next best thing, then you have effectively shot yourself in the foot. I _never_ take someone's word for it when they refer someone to me. Due diligence at all times.

When you are interviewing people, never take their résumé or application at face value. People lie and embellish on these things all the time. If you see things that don't make sense, don't be afraid to dig deeper. Be direct, but kind. For example, if you see that a person has a two-year gap in their employment, you need to understand why. Chances are that they will give you an answer that is designed to paint themselves in the best possible light, yet the truth has a somewhat darker side. I discover things in interviews all of the time that I would never have known had I not dug deeper than what they wanted me to know. Interviewing is a skill that must be honed and developed and it takes practice. Unfortunately, there will be times when you do your best to make a well informed decision, and you get burned. Look for the cues that you missed, and apply them to future interviews.

Recently, I had a manager pass a candidate on to me. Within about two minutes I learned all kinds of terrible things about this person that would have caused me to pass on a second interview. When I presented these things to him, he asked me "Well, do you want me to call him a liar in the interview?" Well, um, YEAH! Don't do it in so many words and don't be rude but hell yes! You have to get to the bottom of the things that do not make sense and if you are not getting the answers that are going to make you comfortable adding this person to your team, then cut 'em loose right now. Save yourself and your team a whole bunch of grief down the road. I call it dodging bullets. Remember, hiring new talent is not about you. It is all about the team you have now, and bringing on the best people to enhance or compliment your team. If you hire carelessly, you and your team can slide backwards pretty fast. Be thorough and be particular.

If you start getting answers that point to consistent issues such as emotional instability, poor stress tolerance, insubordination, frequent job hopping and long periods of unemployment, then pass. Dave Ramsey says in his Entrée Leadership Podcast, "Don't hire crazy". End the interview politely as soon as you make the decision not to hire them, and be hospitable and let them know you aren't hiring them so they don't call you relentlessly for weeks until they finally "get the hint". You can even let them know why if you want to.

Check out http://www.manager-tools.com. The hosts Mark Horstman and Mike Auzenne recently reinforced and validated this long held practice for me in one of their podcasts. You do not want to be seen as the company or the manager that strings people along, and you do not want your time and energy wasted by frequent follow up calls from someone who felt they did well in the interview.

I once interviewed a young man—we will call him Todd. Todd showed up to the interview in our uniform. That impressed me. But, his uniform was very disheveled and wrinkled. He looked pretty bad. In the interview, he did not wow me. He seemed nice, but he had clearly not given much thought to his answers or the reasons he wanted to work for me. He had no concept of what hospitality truly meant, and when I asked him what he could do to improve as a server, his reply was that he could "probably be better about filling drinks and stuff".

I did not hire him, and I told him why not. It sounded something like this: I ended the interview as I always do with the question, "Do you have any questions for me?" He said that he did not.

I said, "Well Todd, I am not going to hire you. And if you are open to some feedback I will tell you why not. Would you be open to that?" He seemed like a kid who might get something out of the feedback, otherwise I would have just ended things and told him I wasn't going to hire him. He said he was open to hearing why.

I explained, "In my restaurant, we are very focused on details, in fact there are ten tiny details that we expect our servers to execute on every table, on top of the normal steps of service. You wore our uniform which is impressive, but your shirt is very wrinkly and your pants are dirty and frayed, this does not tell me that you have an eye for detail. In the interview you did not demonstrate to me that you have a true understanding of hospitality and I did not get the sense that you are a young man who spends much time, thought or energy on things you can do to be a better server. I have a team of really great people, and if I hire someone, I am going to hire someone who respects that level of detail and the work that my team has put into making these things a reality on every shift. Do you understand?" He asked me to elaborate on a few points, which I happily did. We shook hands and he left with me thanking him for his time and wishing him good luck. I even told him that the door wasn't closed, but to please keep us in mind as his skill and experience developed.

A few days later, that young man came back— unannounced—in a perfectly polished uniform and asked for me. He said, "Sir, I just wanted to come back by and tell you that I really think if you gave me a chance that I would impress you. I really love the restaurant that you have here and I would truly appreciate the opportunity to show you what I can do."

After another brief interview focused solely on the things he flubbed on the first time, I hired him on the spot. His mental flexibility and ability to learn impressed me. His courage impressed me; it took guts to come back after the frank rejection I gave him. I highly value courage.

On the other hand, when you have decided to hire someone, you should also let them know. Or at least let them know the next steps. My company encourages a two interview process. I am the final decision maker, but my managers are the ones who have to supervise the people I decide to hire. If I perform the initial interview and know that the person is someone I want on my team, I almost always set the second interview out of respect for their department and relationships. If it is someone I think we should hire, I let them know. If it is someone we are going to hire, I let them know that too. When you have a new team member coming on, they need to understand the chain of command and authority. If I give them the impression that the department manager doesn't matter and I call all the shots, how well do you think that department manager is going to be able to run his or her department?

As a GM, I really like having the final interview. I train my managers by sitting down with them afterwards and interviewing them about the candidate. I ask them questions I would ask in the first interview. If they know the answers, I let them know they did a good job. If they don't, I ask them to find out before they schedule the second interview with me. It saves a lot of time and headaches avoiding second interviews that won't go anywhere. When you do have a second interview, don't rehash the first one. It is a waste of time and you look unprofessional. You and the person doing the first interview should talk before the second interview is executed and you should know all of the answers to all of the first interview questions.

Also, if you have a great applicant walk through your door, then interview them immediately. You do not want them going to work next door with the manager that values people more than you do because you were too rigid in your interview scheduling policies and procedures. It's ok to bend the rules to get great talent on your team. If you like them, then tell them so. Set up a second interview, if necessary, also immediately if you have another manager in the building. Good people are really difficult to find. Don't allow yourself to lose one because of some perceived time constraint.

And finally, after you have been through the interview process, **_always_** check references. There is a really big myth out there that managers all around are blowing way out of proportion. The myth is that you can't ask certain questions of a reference. That is just not true. You can ask whatever you want of the reference as long as it pertains to their job and not protected status such as race, religion, sexual preferences, age, etc. You can legally ask a reference anything you can legally ask an applicant. It is entirely up to the reference what they deem appropriate to answer. You can learn so much about a person this way, and you can dodge a lot of bullets.

Recently I checked a reference of a server applicant. I was on the fence anyway, leaning toward hiring her after the interview. I felt like I didn't have all of the facts or enough information though, so I checked references. I called the first reference that she had listed and introduced myself and why I was calling. I asked if he would be willing to answer a few questions regarding the person in question. The man seemed sheepish at first, and he said, "I am not sure what I can say." I simply said, "Sir, one professional to another, I don't want you to say anything you aren't comfortable with, but you can legally say anything that is true about her work performance as long as it does not pertain to a protected status."

He unloaded.

I did not hire the girl. Let's just say I dodged a cannonball on that one.

In this process, it is important to trust, but not to act entirely on, your instincts. Your instincts are there for a reason. But it isn't smart to rely on them solely. Gather your data, check your references and make a fact based decision. If you have a "bad gut feel", that is important too. With practice you will learn to better identify why you have that feeling and when and how heavily to weigh that in your decision making. Practice is important. You should interview constantly—even when you are not hiring. Many contend—and I agree—*especially* when you are "not hiring"! It is much better to bring in a top notch rock star that you didn't need than to settle for a mediocre tuba player when you are desperate. (To be clear, I have nothing personal against tuba players.)

Check in with Mark and Mike at Manager Tools again, they have a really great podcast on how to ask probing questions of a reference and they talk about how to start small and build up to the really big questions. Manager Tools in general is a very valuable resource for any manager, regardless of level or tenure, to help you sharpen your skills and understand and develop the subtleties of great leadership. I am a huge fan, and I have been listening to them for a little over a year now, and they have helped me a lot. In fact, I refer every internal leadership candidate to the

Manager Tools podcasts as one of the first steps in their development along with a reading list based on their current developmental needs, aptitudes and skill level.

CHAPTER THIRTY-THREE

HOW MUCH WOULD YOU PAY FOR AN EMPTY CHAIR?

As an owner, manager, cook, server, host, busboy, or dishwasher, the sight of an empty chair in your dining room should be mortifying! This is true for any time of day, but particularly during peak business hours. This chapter is really more for restaurateurs than any other business, so if you are a bank teller, you'd be okay skipping this one.

The saying goes, that an empty chair is the most expensive thing in any restaurant. And it is true. The principle holds for any industry although your measurement might not be a chair.

Your goal as a team member, manager, or owner should be to fill in the gaps in the day or week where fewer guests are around but the fact is, you will probably always have some slow times. You must learn to maximize the flow of guests into your dining room at peak times, the level of service and hospitality your guests receive at these times, and always be fearful of an empty chair.

This concept is called Through Put. It is essentially the science of how you make money by increasing and following the flow of business from the front door, through the guest experience, and back out again.

There are a whole range of theories and studies about this, but I will tell you what I have learned in my experience in casual dining and try to wrap it up in as neat a bow as possible. Your company will have training on this in more detail, almost certainly. If they don't, then Google it.

As an owner or manager, consider utilizing a strict three table section policy. This may not be appropriate for your location or concept, so make that decision amongst yourselves. The benefits can be great, but again, just make sure it fits your business model. Most large corporate chains have a strict policy on this that is so strict, any manager caught running a server with more than three tables will be terminated on the spot. A bit extreme, for my blood, and that's precisely why I work where I do.

If, as a server, you are afraid of having a three table station, then get better at math. As long as you are busy, you can make as much if not much more money from three tables than you can four or five. Your restaurant will be able to seat more guests and faster if you are working a three table station. You will likely get more turns in rotation to make up for the "lost table", and you will be able to provide a much more attentive level of hospitality, thereby increasing your tip percentage as well. Further, since your level of attentiveness and hospitality is higher, guest loyalty will thus be stronger and your restaurant will be busier more often. If you know you are going to get 5% of a pie, wouldn't you want it to be a pretty big pie? Trust me, it works.

As a manager, if you are on a wait at the front door and you have empty seats in the dining room, I want you to go find a nice quiet area of the restaurant where you can remove your head from your hindquarters. Slap yourself briskly across the face too, please. Make it quick! You have a restaurant to run.

First, stop by the kitchen to let them know that they have a large pop on the way and to get ready. Motivate them and get them charged up. They may cuss you for a bit, but once you master this (it is more art than science and takes a good deal of practice), then you and your team can really have a lot of fun with it! After you give the kitchen the courtesy heads up, then promptly return to your front door and with the help of your hosts (who will not understand what you are doing at first, but they will soon get it) get every damn table in your dining room seated as quickly as you can trying not to double seat any servers. Be quick and decisive. Before you leave the host, make sure that person understands that they must bus and reset each table as each group leaves and have a new guest there within a minute of the last departure.

Then, move to the dining room and make certain that your servers are all doing well, all tables have been greeted and everything is going smoothly. Make sure your servers are not collecting multiple orders and "sandbagging" the kitchen which will create chaos. Then promptly get to the bar to see if you can help get beverages ready for the influx of guests that just ordered drinks. Help there for a few minutes, but don't be too long.

Next get to the kitchen and help relieve pressure there, on multiple stations if you need to, but do not get in the way. Again, your time is precious, so do not overstay your welcome. Move on within a few minutes. Next, help the expo get the food out of the window and make sure everyone is running food as a top priority over all other things. As soon as that round of food is in the dining room, start working the tables. Make sure everyone is happy and has everything they need.

Next, make sure all side-work is caught up and the restrooms are clean. It doesn't hurt to take a peek at the back door to make sure the building is secure and check the walk-in for prep levels so you can be certain you are prepared for the rest of the business coming in. I'd recommend checking in with your dish guy or gal too and make sure that he or she is having as much fun as you are, and see if they need something cold to drink.

214

Once you have made this round through your restaurant, do it again. And again. Refer to The Shark Theory. The whole process shouldn't take more than ten or fifteen minutes, hitting every area.

Notice how we followed the logical flow of business from the front door, to the dining room, to the bar, to the kitchen and finally buttoned things up with a check on the restrooms and side work. Another common saying in this business, I heard it from Jim Sullivan, is that "If you aren't serving the guest, then you'd better damn well be serving someone who is." Help your team members be successful by serving them in their roles and relieving pressure where and when you see it.

It is worth noting that this pattern should never stop. As long as you are in the building you should make frequent passes through your Figure 8. A very common trap that people in any position fall into is that they let up when it is slower. It is not at all uncommon to get most of your guest complaints from periods of time that are very slow. It is natural and easy to let your guard down at these times, make certain to coach your teams on this and set a good example yourself.

I mentioned earlier that this is somewhat of an art form. I have worked with managers that are perfectly comfortable going on a wait when there are open tables available. Typically these are not solution based thinkers and they have trouble seeing the scenario where you can both seat aggressively, (here is that cool

215

word...) AND be successful. If you seat too fast, you can crush the kitchen. Too slow, you lose money.

There is a balance, and it works. You must be willing and able to figure it out and you must be willing to try and fail before you succeed. Let your team in on the secret though. Surprises can be great, but sometimes they can be really, really bad. You still have a brand to protect, so keep that in mind too along with sales building.

At the end of the day, your team can handle more than they tell you, and so can you. Eliminate excuses and make it happen.

CHAPTER THIRTY-FOUR

MAKE IT FUN! (OR HIRE SOMEONE WHO CAN)

There's that pesky word, "or". Work should be enjoyable, especially in the restaurant business. As a leader, it is your responsibility to make it a fun environment.

This has always been a struggle for me. I have gotten decently good at it, but my strengths tend to gravitate towards getting deep in the numbers side of things. I really enjoy analyzing data and figuring out why things work. That is not inherently fun for most people.

I recognize this about myself, and not only do I work hard at overcoming the weakness on a personal level, I hire towards that weakness. When I interview someone, I want to know that they have a good sense of humor. I want to know what they do for fun both at work, and in their private life. I ask questions like,

"What were you listening to when you pulled in here today?" Or, "what do you do for fun/to relieve stress", etc. I want to make sure that the people I bring on are cool, and fun, and interesting. That makes creating fun so much easier for me as a numbers nerd.

It's okay not to be 100% focused on fun, but if you know you are that kind of person, please respect that not everyone is. Most people want to know that they will enjoy coming to work every day. You want to be that place! If you choose not to be, some of the best, most hospitable and entertaining people will choose to go work somewhere that is.

If you know you have areas where you are not strong, look for those traits when selecting your Team Members, assistant managers and team leaders.

In short, if you can't do it. Hire those who can. It's okay not to be everything, but be careful that you don't get in the way of the people who compliment the gaps in your work habits and leadership style. This goes for fun, or any other area where you might not be fully rounded like analytics, motivation, or knowledge.

CHAPTER THIRTY-FIVE

FEEDBACK

As a leader of a business, relationship building is your primary and most powerful and important skill. As with golf, clubs are designed to do most of the work for you as long as you have taken the time to develop a good swing. If the ability to build and develop valuable relationships with people is your swing, then feedback, coaching and one-on-ones are some of your clubs. It does you absolutely ZERO good to have a nice bright shiny set of Calloway's, if you have no idea how to swing them!

There are a billion resources out there on how to deliver effective feedback. There are a billion tools out there to help you have effective one-on-ones. Again, I am going to suggest you look up Manager Tools on your iPod, or check out http://www.manager-tools.com because their take on this really helped me and I refer all of my new managers to this great, and seemingly limitless, resource. The fact is, they will teach this and other management principles and practices to you better than most people can or will.

There are really great books for you to read, there are mentors you can talk to. I am not going to give you all of the ins and outs, as usual, but I will share with you some things that I have learned and have worked well for me.

First, you have to share time with your people. I have learned from Mark and Mike, and the rest of the team at Manager Tools, that one-on-ones are a great way to do that. If you are a department manager, especially in a high volume restaurant, you probably won't be able to do one-on-ones with your entire team on a weekly basis. It isn't unheard of, but it takes a lot of time and you do have a business to run. But, it is completely feasible to have a very productive meeting of twenty minutes or so with all of your team members once a month. If you have thirty team members, that is one or two a day accounting for your time off each month. Time well spent. You should consider building this into your routine.

Mostly, your meetings should focus on the team member. You should focus on whatever they want to talk about whether it is business related or not. Take the time to get to know them. Be patient. Listen, reflect, and paraphrase. Let them know you are listening and that you care. Congratulate them on wins, answer their questions and address their concerns. Take notes, too. I have a separate notebook where I keep all of my notes from meetings with team members or managers. I keep a list of items that we agree need to happen and I attach dates to time sensitive things and those dates find their way into my calendar so that I can follow up, or so I don't forget the things that I am responsible for. I will interject very little into these meetings and I do not enter them with an agenda outside of one or maybe two things I would like to discuss. My items are usually goal related and I present them in about ten minutes or less at the very end of the meeting, and ask for their help in achieving those things.

You can not be a good leader if you are not well informed. As a department leader, you should have a good working knowledge where each member of your team stands in the performance metrics that are vital to the success of your team.

As a manager, you have to be a person who knows people. Not every person is going to require the same approach. You have to be the chameleon and be able to change based upon the individual you are dealing with at the time.

If you are dealing with an underperforming team member, get *their* ideas on what they can improve on, and how. If you have hired well, and you have taken the time to build a good rapport with them, this should be pretty easy. After they offer some ideas, have them Feed the Egg and come up with a plan for the ultimate solution. Train them to be a solution-based thinker! Set a date to follow up on the plan with the team member and then hold to it.

Again, you are asking permission, detailing behaviors/results, outlining what success looks like, and asking for commitment to change, and following up.

Now, in restaurants you are also going to be doing a lot of real time feedback and coaching. You are going to be managing twenty to thirty people per shift in a fast paced, high stress environment.

You have to know your team.

You have to know who can handle the added pressure of you giving them the proverbial boot in the ass, and who will crumble into a sea of tears.

You must be the person who knows just exactly what to say and how to say it to each individual to get them back on track. You need to know who might need a second to cool off, or who might need to hear a quick joke, or who just needs a little help. You have to be in tune with everything from the front to back door and keep your team performing admirably and be a gracious host for your guests.

This takes *a lot* of practice and time. You really have to know your crew. I have guys on the line that I can walk up to and whisper things that would get me sued or fired if I said it to the wrong person, but it gets *them* fired up. I have team members who need to be told in real time and in no uncertain terms to get it together. While other team members would break down in tears if I said the same thing to *them*.

Some team members just need a pat on the back, or to be told that it's okay, or to see you work or smile or laugh. Sometimes all I do is make a face at someone who seems to be stressed out. The responsibility for a successful shift, and restaurant, rests directly on your shoulders. If your team knows you well, and knows that you care for them, then the road ahead will be much easier. You cannot let the weight and pressure of running a business distract you from doing the one and only thing your team needs from you—leading them.

CHAPTER THIRTY-SIX

MANAGING CONFLICT

Managing conflict is difficult, especially when you are managing it between two people who have most likely not developed the interpersonal skills to do this on their own. It is different when the people you are trying to get to work well together are mature professionals who have a sense of responsibility to the common mission or goal. Pride, misperceptions and hurt feelings are a tremendous obstruction.

Sometimes, you are dealing with two people who are not well equipped to manage the conflict in a productive way. And, sadly, workplace violence is a common and real threat that you must consider when dealing with these issues. Your company will undoubtedly have training on this issue for you and I am sure they have their own set of policies and procedures. Follow those carefully and you will be fine.

Here's my advice if you find yourself in one of these delicate situations. If you have a conflict between two team members, you need to evaluate quickly whether that conflict is a minor disagreement, a potential threat, or an impending threat. First of all, don't get involved if you don't have to. A minor disagreement should be able to be settled between two grown-ups without you. Coach the team members individually on how to approach the situation.

If you do need to get involved, things can be handled with a mediated conversation. This should end in a hand shake, a mutual apology and an understanding of each other's viewpoint. Recently in my restaurant I had two team members that were at each other's throats—verbally, not physically. We were pretty busy so sending either home was not a feasible option at the time. I pulled each one into the office individually and asked about their side of the story. I listened and asked questions designed to get them to at least consider the other person's point of view. I let them know that I was going to bring them together as soon as possible to discuss the problem, but until then to avoid one another. I let them know that I expected the confrontation to be constructive and respectful. Then I kept an eye on them. This gave them some time to let the anxiety of the impending confrontation to sink in and mellow a bit.

At the first opportunity, I brought them together. I said, "Look, I know you both better than you know each other, and I know you are both good people. I also know that you each have stressful jobs in different ways, and that if you take a little time to understand each other's viewpoint, that you would be more courteous to one another. Now, I am not going to tell you what to say, and you don't have to apologize to each other if you don't mean it, but I do have some ground rules for the conversation. First, you must speak respectfully to each other. No name calling and speak only in terms of behaviors that the other person can change to help you. Second, no interrupting, no matter how much you disagree. Third, I want you to discuss an alternative way you can discuss your problems with each other when they arise so you don't blow up at each other".

I got their agreement to abide by the rules (I had already planted these seeds, so they had already thought about it for a while), and let them talk. They discussed the matter, disagreed respectfully, both apologized, shook hands, and went back to work. They aren't perfect at dealing with each other still, but they got to know each other a little better, and that is a good step in the right direction.

These team members can go back to work with each other, but keep an eye on them.

If you get into a situation where two parties are disagreeing and you pull them aside to talk, and one of the parties is indignant, nasty, antagonistic, snarky, confrontational, violent, aggressive or any combination or variation of those things, you have a very serious situation that takes some skill to diffuse.

First, ask the person who is being reasonable to excuse themselves and get another manager to sit down with you before moving on. You need to send the other person home immediately and let them know why. This is an impending threat, and you are in for it if you let them both stay with one another, and you are putting yourself in danger if you do not handle this with care and tact. Also, let them know that before they can return to work, they need to have a meeting with you and your general manager. Leave detailed notes in your manager log book about the incident and get statements from any witnesses to the incident.

If there is violence of any kind, follow your company's policy, but the best bet is to get both parties out of the restaurant. If it is mutual violence such as a fight, both parties should be terminated. If it is an assault, as in one person strikes another and the other does not retaliate, then you need to terminate the offending party and I call the police to file a report.

Never put yourself in harm's way. If you do not feel comfortable handling a situation, call the cops. No one expects you to be a hero and break up a fight like a bouncer.

Now, if you get into a situation where two team members are disagreeing and it is clear they are going to be an issue working together, separate them if you can, but if not send one of them home and schedule a time after everyone has had a while to cool off where you can all sit down and discuss the matter. There may not be an impending threat, but the potential is there for this to escalate beyond your control.

As with most things, this takes training, practice and experience to master. It would be awesome if you could just make all the perfect hiring decisions and everyone would get along like peas in a pod, but that just isn't the case. You are going to have egos clash and at some point it is going to get heated. How you handle the situation will say a lot to your team about your leadership.

CHAPTER THIRTY-SEVEN

CRISIS MANAGEMENT

As a manager and business leader of men and women, at some point in your career something really wild is going to happen that you did not expect and no one in their right mind would have imagined preparing you for. You have to be quick on your feet, and be able to make fast decisions that are in the best interest of your patrons, your team, and your business.

When I was first starting out in my restaurant management career, I remember all of the things that I used to worry about. They were valid concerns. Real crisis, such as what do I do if there is a fire, tornado, earthquake, robbery, a guest having a heart attack, slips and falls, etc. Things like that used to keep me up at night. You want to know what the very first "crisis" I had to manage was? Every cube of ice and every drop of water in my restaurant turned a terrible brownish-red color. One of my servers said, "Tony, you may want to go look in the ice bin." So, being the obedient rookie manager that I was, I did. Our ice bin was an old double sided behemoth that would make and hold a literal ton of ice in less than twenty-four hours. And the top ten inches of ice were almost all brownish-red.

Of course, these things never happen at ten o'clock on a Monday night. Nope. Seven thirty Friday night is when these things always happen. Busiest shift of the week, every time. My restaurant at the time seated about two hundred and fifty people. Every seat was full and there was a line out the door. And, in North Georgia, people like their water with lemon. And they like it a lot.

I grabbed two things, cash and a hostess. I sent both up the street to the big box store with instructions to come back with as many bottles of water and bags of ice as she could buy with two hundred bucks. God bless her, she came back with about fifteen of those big, blue water cooler style bottles! Good thinking, but sort of a pain in the ass to pour out of. We had just gotten a forced shipment of new meat in these huge Styrofoam coolers packed in dry ice. We lined these with garbage bags and put all of our ice in them. We worked like that the rest of the night, having to make a couple of emergency runs for ice, but we made it happen.

Another time, I was sitting in the office toward the end of the night, and one of my servers comes in and says that they need me at the bar right away. The restaurant that I ran at the time was known as a late night hangout and we were pretty much the only game in town after ten o'clock.

So after ten, the families would mosey out, and the drunks would stumble in. We called it shift change, for obvious reasons, but really the whole demeanor of the place changed. It was always a *fun* place to work, but after ten it also got *interesting*. There were a lot of fights and I was literally a not-so-well-paid bouncer many nights. Because of this, I always carried a 3 D-cell Mag-Lite in the waistband of my slacks. Anyone who has ever handled one of these guys knows that it might as well be a metal baseball bat that lights up on the end.

Armed with my flashlight-bat, I got up from my paperwork and headed for the dining room. As I exited the kitchen and entered the bar area I noticed a large group of angry people circling a man sprawled face-down on the horseshoe shaped bar, near the service well. I noticed right away that the inner most circle of people had blood smeared on their shirts and they were equal parts pissed, disgusted and curious. As I breached the circle, I noticed now that the face-down man was somewhat elderly and not only lying face down in a pool of, but also covered—and I mean covered—in blood.

I was not sure if the crowd had taken things into their own hands and I was now becoming witness to a murder, I didn't know if this guy just killed his whole family, I didn't know if he had just shot himself. All kinds of things were running through my mind.

231

I asked one of the bartenders what had happened and he told me he had come in that way and stumbled into a whole group of people and face planted right where he was now. I asked if he had been served anything, of course the answer was, "hell no".

I approached the man cautiously, and gently touched his shoulder. I said, "Sir, are you alright?" The man jerked his head up and looked at me with his bloody, weather worn face and crystal blue, bloodshot and glassy eyes. The sweet stench of stale booze hit me in the face and the old, bloody man struggled to his feet. The circle of blood-smeared shirts widened slightly. He had cuts all over and he was bleeding so badly from some of them that I was shocked he could stand at all. With clenched teeth and fists he squared off at me, locked my gaze, and snarled, "You don't know nuthin about no goddam Vietnam, do you boy?"

Oh. Shit.

"No sir, I do not know a damn thing about no Vietnam."

"I ought to fucking kill you right here!"

Okay, this is escalating quickly. Did I mention—Oh shit?

This old vet was standing between me and the door, so I began backing my way around the bar in an attempt to get him to the door the long way. He followed. Now, my kitchen crew was awesome. They were young and big and always eager to help break up a fight when the situation arose. One of these guys was a six foot nine, three hundred pound black dude with dreadlocks and gang tattoos nicknamed "Runt". Having been put on red alert by my service team, as we approached the kitchen entrance, my guys were there. Runt stepped in and started to grab the guy, when I said "Be careful Runt, he's bleeding!" My smallest hostess could not have matched the squeal he let out when he saw that! It was hysterical in spite of the gravity of the situation! So, anyways, Runt is out of the fight.

I had a preset signal with my bartender to let him know it was time to call the police. I gave that signal, *urgently*. This old guy kept marching toward me, and I kept marching toward the front door. He was snarling and threatening me and coming closer and closer. As we approached the door, I said, "Look sir, all I want is for you to get home tonight and the police are going to be here any second. You'd better leave."

With that, he bolted for the exit. Our restaurant was located at the bottom of a hill coming off of a long bridge that spanned railroad tracks and headed downtown. As the man exited, about five police cars came screaming over the bridge and down the hill veering into our parking lot. I followed the man out the door as he staggered downhill toward his parked car.

He was driving a big, old '68 Pontiac four-door with a rusty iron trailer hitch sticking off of the rear bumper about a foot. I could see where this was going, and it wasn't good. As the police neared, he began trying to run. He lost his footing and took about two or three big cart wheeling steps and finally lost his battle with gravity, face planting directly on that big trailer hitch of his, crumpling to a lifeless ball, momentum wedging him under the rear-end of his car. It was pretty grotesque. And scary. I was still only a first year restaurant manager.

Come to find out, this old guy was a repeat visitor of the county jail. He was also an alcoholic and a hemophiliac. A bad combination.

No amount of training can prepare you for something like that. My goal was to get the guy out of the restaurant and make sure my team and my guests were safe. In a different situation this guy could have been a guest too, though. I did not want him to go to jail, and I certainly did not want him to be injured further. When it comes down to it, we all make our decisions in life and we all have to pay for, or reap the benefits of those decisions.

So, be prepared for the tornado and the fire and the robbery and all the things that your company can tell you might happen someday. But keep your wits sharp and your eyes open because I promise you the unexpected and un-*expectable* will happen. Every restaurateur or barkeep has stories that would shock, amaze and entertain you.

CHAPTER THIRTY-EIGHT

GUEST RECOVERY

To me this is so easy and so screwed up by most managers. Look, you have to care. If you don't, your guests will know and your team will know. If you don't, please go look for other work. I have bad days where my heart or my head just isn't in the game just like everyone else, but if you are a good person, you have to set aside how you are feeling to address the feelings of others. How terrible is it to allow a person to sit at your table and allow them to feel neglected, or cheated or in any way offended by the actions of your team? It's pretty terrible. And, it's thoughtless and selfish too.

This job, if you haven't figured out by now, is not about you. It is about other people and your power to make the world a better and happier place.

Guest recovery is simple and it doesn't start with the guest. It starts with your team. I mean that in more ways than one really.

First, you have to empower your team to fix mistakes without you. If you are a manager who insists that your team members find you and get permission from you before doing what they think is right to fix a problem, then good luck to you. Why would you take precious moments away from the process of guest recovery? You have to train your team how to handle situations and then you have to empower them to fix it. If they make a mistake, it's okay. Teach them to learn from their mistakes, and move on.

I once filled in for a manager at a different restaurant in a company I worked for. It was clear that he does not train his team to do this. Through the entire shift I had servers come up to me telling me that I needed to fix their problems for them. This is how I handled it. A server, we'll use Sally, approached me and said, "We are out of mashed potatoes, so you need to go to table eight and talk to them."

"Okay, sure. What steps have you already taken to fix the problem?"

"I don't fix problems, that's your job."

"Sally, no it isn't. That is your table and your tip. Did you try suggesting some of our other great sides?"

236

"No."

"I tell you what. Why don't you go offer them some of the new corn dish we just introduced? Let them know it's great and if they don't love it, you will bring them something they do love. I will get it started from the kitchen and deliver it personally and make sure I make you look good doing it. How does that sound?"

"Okay."

She was hesitant and unsure. She had never been told she could do that before. The guest agreed to the corn and I did what I said I would do. I delivered the corn and spoke with her table. It was a nice couple in their sixties. "Folks, here is your corn. I know Sally feels terrible that we did not have the mashed potatoes you wanted, but she asked if we could substitute the corn and I thought it was a great suggestion. Will you let me know what you think of it?"

"Sure."

"My apologies for not having your potatoes ready. Enjoy your meal."

I checked back with them shortly and they loved it. As they should have, it was an amazing dish! Afterward, I pulled Sally aside and apologized to her for running out of potatoes and asked if the couple was enjoying themselves. She said they were having a great time. They also ordered coffee and dessert and tipped her very well, thanking her for the suggestion of the corn.

The second thing you want to do is to make sure that the situation is not creating too much stress for your team. When routines get derailed, it is easy for tensions to rise and people to lose focus. You have to be able to keep things on track. Sometimes it takes finesse and touch, and sometimes it takes brute strength and awkwardness. Let your team know exactly what needs to happen for everything to get back to normal and let them know the timeframe it needs to happen in.

After your team has enacted a solution to the problem, they should know to get the manager on duty involved right away. As a manager, you should always try to have meaningful interactions with every guest, and absolutely with a guest recovery. Never let a problem walk out of your restaurant a problem. Recovery is going to be different for every guest. If you take a cookie cutter approach, you will be seen as insincere and you would have been better off not visiting the table. Here is my approach:

1. I find out what the problem was and where we are in the solution process. I want to know specifically how many minutes until the guest is happy.

2. I approach the table and introduce myself by name and title.

3. I address the offended party and the person who looks the most pissed off. Note that these are not always the same person.

4. Please do not play dumb. They know what your mistake was. You know what your mistake was, even if it wasn't "really" a mistake. If the guest thinks it was, then it was. Accept it, deal with it, embrace it, get over it.

I acknowledge the mistake and accept full blame, and I add something about the server being all over the issue. Always make your team look like the heroes that they are. The guests love it, and your team loves it. Never ask something obtuse like, "What seems to be the trouble?" A) You are opening yourself up for a much longer table visit than you need to have, and B) It's insulting and it makes you look ill-informed and ill-prepared, and well, stupid. If you really don't know or understand what the guest is looking for, then frame it in a way that disarms the guest's discomfort or anger.

5. I am empathetic and always slightly more upset than the guest about the situation. If they think it's no big deal, I think it's terrible. If they think it's terrible, I find it appalling and unprofessional. If they think it's appalling and unprofessional, I jump up and down like Yosemite Sam and fire the first person that walks by...ah, well you get the idea. It is worth noting that as I write things like this, I am always picturing someone taking me seriously and jumping up and down screaming while holding

hands with a guest in the middle of a dining room somewhere. It's pretty funny. At least in my head it is. Anyway...

6. I apologize (sincerely) and let them know where we are in the process of recovery.

7. I let them know what I am personally doing to help the server get it out as fast as possible.

8. I repeat my name and offer to get them something else to snack on while they wait for the corrected food.

9. I personally deliver the food once it is corrected. I deliver a full plate dressed out with fresh sides.

10. I am gauging the guest's temperature the whole time. How mad are they?

11. I ask if there is anything further I can do to offer them a better dining experience.

12. I go to the server and ask them what they think we should do for them.

13. I always "over-recover". Always comp the item on which the error was made, or give them a gift card for their next visit. Manage your comp line by not making mistakes, not by under-recovering.

I have a little private rule that I will share with you. When I am performing a guest recovery, I always want the guest to feel just the slightest bit guilty about the lengths to which we go to make it right. Not too much. Just a little. I know, I know, we want to make people feel warm and at home—don't preach to me! I'm the one writing the book here!

The way I look at it, if they feel just a teensy bit guilty about how well we recovered the situation, then that will come out when they tell the story later. The last thing out of their mouth will be, "...but you wouldn't believe how well they handled the situation!" Instead of, "...and the manager never even stopped by the table!"

You will encounter guests from time to time who will be insulted if you comp their food. Really insulted. In this case, leave it alone. But give them a gift card to come back and visit.

Danny Meyer, famed restaurateur and creator of Union Square Cafe in New York City, wrote a book a few years back called *Setting the Table: The Transforming Power of Hospitality in Business*. This is a fantastic book for any segment of business that deals with people. In his book he talks about "writing the last great chapter" when you make a mistake. This is the central thinking behind my concept of over recovery and this is critical when dealing with an angry or upset guest. Also critical is empathy. I placed the chapter "Understanding the Passion" at the beginning of this book for a reason, and that is because you must honestly be able to put yourself in the guest's position.

241

If you haven't read Meyer's book, I highly recommend it. Mr. Meyer has an unmatched passion for hospitality and an eye for detail that gave me some really great ideas at about the midpoint of my management career thus far.

CHAPTER THIRTY-NINE

FIRING YOUR GUEST

Most companies don't train their people how to fire an employee, much less a guest. It's not something that we want to encourage, obviously. We are in this to make money. But unfortunately there will be times in your career where you may have to ask a guest to leave your establishment.

Some segments of the market are more prone to that for obvious reasons. When there is alcohol involved, it is easy for things to get out of hand if you choose to let it. Bars and nightclubs can have fights, or guests can be over served. But sometimes you just run into a jerk who wants to verbally abuse the server, bartender, hosts and management team.

Sometimes it is really cut and dried, but nobody ever told me how to do it. Early in my career, I was under the impression that the guest is always right and that you should never, ever kick a guest out. You should grin and bear it and wait the situation out.

Now let's start with the statement "the guest is always right". Bullshit. The guest is frequently wrong, and can be uneducated, ill-informed, hostile, rude, abusive and self-entitled.

It is our job to create hospitality and to serve and cater to the needs and desires of each guest that comes into our establishment. That does not mean that you are subject to endure the hostility of someone who has misplaced their anger or over estimated their authority in the current situation.

Now, as a rule, you should be prepared to absorb a pretty huge amount of abuse. That is the job we are in. We have chosen hospitality because we want to make people's day better. That means that from time to time, we are going to encounter a guest that is just in a nasty mood and wants to take it out on us. Maybe *they* don't even know why, they are just having a bad day. They are heavily biased to the Horrible! end of The Hospitality Ladder. We want to take the frustrated and turn them into the happy. We want the angry turned into the glad. It's our job! If you go kicking out every guest that gets the least bit snippy, you are going to run out of guests pretty fast.

Step 1: Grow (you and your team) a strong back bone.

Step 2: Be an advocate not only for the guest, but for your team.

Step 3: Know where your line is. That is, know what it looks like to you when a guest has overstepped that line. I gotta tell you, your line better be pretty far back. There are a million ways to successfully placate an angry and abusive guest.

Step 4: Know what to do and *say* when that line is crossed. This may require a little role-play.

Step 5: When the line is crossed, protect your team and keep the guests dignity very close to your heart.

In short, this is one of those clubs in your bag that you should never have to use; and, if you do have to use it, it's probably a good idea to think back to your last shot and evaluate what could have prevented you from having to pull it out.

Here are two examples from my past. They both ended up okay, one worked out better than the other—depending on your point of view.

One night my restaurant was very busy. We were on a long wait and pretty much every position was feeling the pinch. I was behind the bar helping them push out a few cocktails when I heard a loud commotion from the dining room floor. As I finished up and started to head that way, one of my hosts met me about half way and said that one of my servers needed help that a guest had her pinned against the wall.

Now, the server in question is one of the sweetest girls you will ever meet. She is about five feet tall and weighs about ninety pounds soaking wet. Not only is she very sweet and kind, she is also one of the best servers that I have ever worked with. As I rounded the corner, I see her in tears, backed against a support post with a red-faced, middle-aged man three times her size shaking his finger in her face and yelling at her. For one, this is so far over my line it's ridiculous. At this point, I do not care what the guest has to say. You absolutely do not treat my team like this. I literally slid into the spot where she was standing and quietly excused her. I am a foot and a half taller than her so the angry patron had to comically reposition himself to shove his finger in my face and said, "And who the fuck are you?"

"I am the General Manager. How can I help you?"

He ranted. Stood there with balled fists and yelling at me in the middle of the dining room. I could feel his spit hitting my face. I let him finish, but to tell you the truth, I have no clue what he said or what he was upset about.

I calmly said, "Sir, I understand you're upset…"

He cut me off and shouted, "Don't fucking tell me 'I understand'! I've been in sales for twenty years, I know all about 'I understand'!" I looked over the man's shoulder at his thoroughly embarrassed teenage daughter.

I smiled at him, and I asked him—very politely—to leave.

246

After a small amount of huffing and puffing, he complied. The rest of the patrons applauded as he left.

Win win! We won in one aspect because we never saw the prick again—to be totally honest—good riddance. The biggest win is the loyalty that I earned from the team. They saw that I would defend them and protect them and that was a big step for me in the leadership of that restaurant, especially with the server involved. She would tell all new team members up until the day I left the company how great of a boss I was and that they could count on me to have their back as long as they did the right things.

Scenario number two. It was a busy Friday lunch and we were on a wait. As I approached the host stand during my figure 8, I noticed a gruff, older man, who is upset. He is yelling and swearing at my hosts. Maybe there are people out there better than me that would handle this differently, but I refuse to tolerate a person yelling and swearing at one of my team members. I don't care how bad we screwed up. There is no call for it.

The gentleman was upset that there was a wait. As I approached, I introduced myself by name and title and asked how I could help. He began swearing at me and jabbing a finger at my host told me to get "this dumbass in line". "Sir," I said, very politely. "I am here to help, but I am going to ask you to stop speaking to my team like that." He shouted, "Then you need to do it!"

I looked him dead in the eye and with an even and calm voice said, "Sir, with all due respect, I would never speak to anyone that way."

He physically shuddered with rage, but he thought for a second before he spoke again. "You know what. You are right. I'm pissed off and out of line. I apologize."

"Thank you for saying so sir. I do want to help you. What would make you happy right this second?"

"I want to sit down and eat!"

"Easy enough. Can you give me a moment to get a table ready for you?" I just happened to see a group getting up from a table behind him.

"Yes."

We cleaned the table quickly and seated him immediately. I made certain his food was perfect and was expedited from the kitchen in a big damn hurry. The gentleman visited my restaurant no less than three times per week after that, including every Friday for two bowls of clam chowder, and he and I became good friends.

This was a win because we got to keep the guest and make a regular of him. He just wanted to be made to feel important, and my inexperienced hosts were struggling with that. It was a win, because I earned more loyalty from my team seeing that I would stand up for them. And, it was a win because I identified a great coaching opportunity to help my host staff be more proactive at the door when quoting their wait times and communicating with guests.

Aside from these two stories, I have only had to remove two other guests from my establishments over the years for being abusive to my team members. I'm not counting when I was a bar manager, there we threw drunks out all the time. But, both of the other situations were when I was a newer manager and at the time it was the right thing to do. Fifteen years is a long time to remember things, and I often look back and wonder if I would have handled those situations the same way now, or if they could have been avoided by a more mature management sensibility, or even better interpersonal skills. Though, in my mind, there is no reason to verbally or physically abuse another human, and especially not one for whom I am responsible for their happiness and wellbeing.

You have to make the judgment call. 99.99% situations should be a win-win. Actively seeking an opportunity to fire a guest is not a good business model, but you should play scenarios like this out in your head and then do everything in your power to prevent them. Practice things you can say to diffuse the situation. When guests are upset, they really just want an advocate. A lot of people aren't very skilled at handling their emotions. If you are skilled at remaining calm and finding the cause of their frustration, the rest isn't very hard. If such situations do arise, you need to handle them with poise. Go in looking for a fight, and you will undoubtedly find one. Go in seeking a mutually beneficial solution, and you will likely find that too.

Just remember that your first responsibility is to your team. They, after all, are the ones caring for the guest.

CHAPTER FORTY

OWNERSHIP

Okay, I am not going to go into all of the nuances that make owning your own place a success. Not that kind of book. I have not yet owned my own business, so there is a lot I do not know. This is advice based on a couple of very important lessons I have learned through experience as a manager that has worked for private small business owners, and maybe a story or two.

I worked for two bars that failed. I have seen dozens of other restaurants and bars fail. I have been part of many openings—successful and otherwise—and I have been around this business a long time. I've seen things, man—I have seen things. Most of these places were owned by relatively smart individuals, some of whom were very successful in other corners of the business world—and they flat out failed and lost their entire life savings at ages where that would be more than just devastating.

If you are considering buying a business in hospitality, here are some sound words of advice that come from many years of experience and observation:

1. Understand that the restaurant and bar business is exceptional and unique in more ways that you can imagine. If you have never worked in the business, think long and hard before you invest a dime. Liking to drink, eat, and enjoying a great bar or restaurant do not make you an expert in any way. Be careful, because if you think your business experience and love of the finer things in life will make you a great bar or restaurant owner, then be prepared to be very disappointed.

2. If you do not have experience, spend a year or two and get some. Yes, you may have been the CEO of your former company, but now you need to go be a dish guy and a cook and a server and even a manager before you invest any money. Really get into the nitty gritty of what makes a person great in each position. You will not be sorry you did. You must understand the beast before you can tame the beast.

3. If you are unable or unwilling to get the experience, hire a trusted professional with the experience to run it—then let them. Too many inexperienced owners try to jump in and micromanage something they do not understand to their own demise. Do not take this to mean you shouldn't hold your GM to performance standards. This still works like any other business that way. Just make sure your financial goals are realistic, and

hold each other accountable to them. If you insist on running it yourself, I respect that, but hire a trusted consultant to be with you the whole way until you get on your feet.

4. Start small. I have seen some very big and very expensive dreams go up in smoke. Start small, and build your way up. You will know when it is time to hit the gas.

5. Don't open until you are 100% ready. If you open half-assed, then you are giving the wrong first impression. If your place is unfinished or you aren't ready, it will show. Set realistic time-bound goals and hit them, but do not be afraid to push the opening back when you realize that you won't be ready. I know this can be short term loss of revenue, but it beats having 500 people running around town talking about your half-assed opening. Be 100% ready, and then do a soft opening. After the soft opening, you work out the kinks and put the finishing touches on things and then advertise your grand opening like a mo-fo. Also, when your grand opening arrives, please do not screw it up.

6. Don't forget what made you successful in the first place. I have seen owners expand, only to completely alter their concept and scratch their heads when things don't work out. It's ok to make some improvements, but if you are going to completely change things up, rename the new place and create a new brand. Don't try to ride the coattails of a successful brand with something totally different because at some point, you are

going to alienate your core clientele. This one is for you George Lucas. I mean really, Jar Jar Binx?

7. Don't cut corners. Be cost conscious, but let quality of products and service guide your decisions over price. You will create so many headaches for yourself and your staff if all you do is beat down on costs. Especially when it comes to construction, HVAC, and Equipment. Think about it, you spend $300,000 on a new place, and people won't come see you in the summer because you didn't spend the extra $5K to get an AC unit that could effectively cool your establishment? Brilliant cost management on your part. It sounds ridiculous, but I have seen it happen.

8. Do not sample your own product. If you do feel the need to have a beer or sandwich, get your wallet out like every other guest.

9. Under no circumstances ever, ever get intoxicated at your own establishment. You can set the policy for employees to be whatever you like, but you don't get to play, sorry. As a bar manager I have had to put the nix on a lot of boneheaded deals my boss made, or break the news to someone they weren't actually hired, when he was wasted. It was a waste of my time and very hard on morale. You do not make good decisions when you are drinking, learn it and live it now. That same guy lost everything, incidentally.

10. Set your business up to protect yourself and your family finances. LLC or LLP are pretty common. Use other people's money when and where you can. You will have to have some form of down payment, but do not leverage your personal finances to set up shop unless you just have too much money, in that case—let's talk.

11. Location is important, kinda. I really believe that *any* location can be successful if it is run and marketed properly. That being said, if you are looking at buying a place where the last five places have flopped, consider picking a new location. Locations that have a revolving door of different bars and restaurants definitely get a stigma attached in the market as being unsuccessful, and it might be better not to have to fight that fight. You can probably think of one or two examples in your own hometown off the top of your head. I appreciate that you have the confidence to give it a go, but carefully consider the gamble.

12. If you are going to spend more than $250,000 on an existing place, consider new construction or building out a new location. You will have to determine on your own whether this makes sense or not, but people often want way too much money for their existing business—and existing problems. Often times people want out because they see some writing on the wall that you may not see, such as a huge downward trend in revenue. Maybe the old owner just doesn't have the spark left to turn it around and some new blood is just what the place needs. Maybe

the market is trending away from that concept or geographical location. Hire the experts to help you figure that out. It will be well worth the investment.

13. Market. Every third sentence out of your mouth should be related to marketing your business. There are a bunch of things that you can do to market your new bar or restaurant but I am here to tell you that the most impactful ones are free, or very cheap. Don't waste a whole lot of time on radio or TV. As you look at expanding and growing your brand, these are options, but at first go cheap. First you need to know who you are marketing to. Fully embrace BSP (Blatant Self Promotion).

14. Be Consistent. Have a vision going into it. Think it through, then see it through. Don't open your doors and then start trying all kinds of goofy gimmicks to build business. Make a good plan, hire great people, and make it happen.

These are obviously not the only things to consider with ownership, but definitely some things that will help you. I cannot stress enough the importance of hiring the experts to help you be successful, but if you are considering this path, it is also important to note that not many people are successful in business by not taking risks.

I encourage you to take risks, be innovative and try things no one else thinks will work, but make your risks very calculated and make sure you have the stones to see it through.

PUTTING IT ALL TOGETHER

At the beginning of this journey, I shared with you some personal things about my life that shaped the way I interact with myself and the world. My struggles pale in comparison to many. There are a lot of people out there who have had it much better than me in many ways, there are a ton of people who have had it much, much worse. I look back at my life thankful for all of the blessings I have been granted and I have few regrets. And, my journey is far from over. Ten years from now, this might be an entirely different book in many ways.

Also, I am not a scientist, therapist, or expert in human psychology. And, most importantly, I am not you.

Your journey will be unique, and it will naturally be more important to you than to anyone else. Only you can take charge of the way that journey goes. In essence, you are driving the car. Get a map, choose your destination, fill up with gas and check the tires, and go. You're not going to get anywhere sitting on the couch feeling depressed or sorry for yourself.

The desired end game here is to be productive and get good results. To make better decisions that lead to a more fruitful and rewarding life. It's not okay just to get by. To be a good citizen of this great country, you must make a contribution and be part of the solution. It's as simple as deciding to do it.

It's embarrassingly simple yet can be terribly difficult. For me it was easy in the sense that when I made the commitment to bettering my life, I rarely strayed from the path. When I decided to forgive myself for my mistakes, and learn from them, it became easier to move forward after them.

Some people will say to start small, but that isn't my style. All along, I knew the things that were holding me back, but there was always an excuse for holding on to the old ways. What I was really saying to myself is that I was afraid to change. I was afraid to be uncomfortable, even though my bad decisions and self destructive behavior were making me the most uncomfortable. I was afraid to fail.

I say start big. Start with the biggest things in your life that are the glaring, bright, gaudy flashing warning signs holding you back. The proverbial low hanging fruit. Take a sledgehammer to your roadblocks and destroy them permanently.

We all look back, and that is healthy I think. Don't ignore your past; you have to deal with those things. My recommendation is that you do what you need to do to deal with the things that cripple, frustrate and bother you. Accept them for what they are, and move on.

Remember, your past is exactly that, your past. No amount of stress, worry, regret, guilt, or sadness will ever change it and you can't ever go back. So why waste your energy on those negative emotions? Imagine trying to drive a car on a cross country journey and spending 80% of your time gazing into your rearview mirror, wishing that you had stopped at the sites that had already passed you by? It wouldn't be a very fun trip, not to mention a rather dangerous one! You'd keep missing all the cool things coming up, and you'd keep seeing them pass in the rearview and regretting you missed them. Keep your eye on the road, and enjoy the ride. The rearview mirror is there if you need to glance at it once in a while.

You *can* control the future though. Every decision you make each day; how you choose to speak to people, how you choose to work, how you choose to react to positive and negative things in your life and at work, it's all up to you. Whether you choose to complain, or act. Those decisions represent you to the world, and trust me, the world will respond accordingly.

When it comes to getting things done, the solution is really easy. Just do it. Act. Make a move. Set a goal, and figure out what steps it will take for you to achieve it and hit the gas. It doesn't get much simpler than that.

Having the right tools helps, so ask around. Talk with the kinds of people who are where you want to be. Read books. Listen to podcasts. Go to school. Visit with a coach or therapist. There are dozens, hundreds, *thousands* of resources at your disposal. Most of them are cheap, if not free. Once you get started, the process takes on a life of its own. Your way of thinking starts to change. Your perspective changes. Your language changes.

Things get pretty exciting after that.

RESOURCES

When getting started and searching for resources, it can be counterproductive to start at the wrong level. For example, if you are an entry level hourly team member who has never read a book about self-improvement or leadership, and you jump in and start reading Good to Great by Jim Collins, you are probably not going to get a lot out of it. Below, I have listed some of the resources that have helped me—especially at the beginning of my journey.

In the beginning, it is important to know yourself, your tendencies, and your strengths and weaknesses before you choose your starting point. So, I recommend taking a personality assessment that is geared toward professional environments. You can do a search on the internet for "professional personality assessments" and get a ton of results. "16 Personalities" is pretty decent free online test. It isn't as eerily accurate as some of the more in depth ones out there, but if you have limited resources, it's a good start.

Ask your boss if your company offers these types of assessments. Many companies have ones that they are partial too. One of the more popular tests out there and the first one I ever took that just nailed me to the tee is DiSC Personality Assessment. It's about thirty bucks worth of spooky, and worth the money if you really want to know the hard truth about yourself. I have taken several of these in my career and it never ceases to amaze me how some shrink from thirty years ago can pin me down so accurately just by asking me a few questions. The key is that you have to answer from your gut and honestly.

There are a few books and other resources that I think everyone should begin with. The book People Skills, by Robert Bolton is a fantastic starting point. It can give you a lot of tools to handle conflict more effectively and learn skills that can help you build stronger relationships both in your personal and professional life.

Next I recommend another classic, The Seven Habits of Highly Effective People by the late Steven Covey. To me, all of these types of book are way too longwinded, and this one is no exception, but it is very good at providing a good foundation on which to build your path to success. The principles presented in this book are some of the best advice you will receive in terms of habits you can easily implement to improve your life. Both People

Skills and Seven Habits are books that I recommend revisiting multiple times throughout your life.

Once you have gotten these two books under your belt, Dale Carnegie has a plethora of books that could be very useful. How to Win Friends and Influence People, and How to Stop Worrying and Start Living are timeless classics that have helped me immensely. He has many other books that could be valuable depending on the type of progress that you are trying to make with yourself.

There are a collection of books, that are quick and easy reads, designed to deliver powerful principles quickly and effectively. Who Moved My Cheese, by Dr. Spencer Johnson is a really good book that can help you adjust to change more easily.

Ken Blanchard has a huge catalog of titles he has authored that are favorites of managers and trainers everywhere. The One Minute Manger, Whale Done, and Raving Fans are a few of my favorites and I would recommend reading them all. Reading all of those books would probably take you about twelve hours.

Since we are on the subject of the great Ken Blanchard, as you continue your diligent quest for more skill and professionalism, check out the CD2 Leadership training they offer at http://www.cd2leadership.com. It is fairly inexpensive, and a really great resource for learning some basics of leadership, goal setting, and relationship building. I like all of Blanchard's training materials for two main reasons: One, they are simple and fun. He keeps you entertained and interested. Two, he delivers all of his messages in very simple and quick packages that are easy to understand and implement immediately. Another cool thing about his website is they will provide you with continuous training and endless newsletters, book titles and other resources to help you through specific challenges you may be facing. The organization is truly passionate about, and focused on, improving the lives of others through effective training. Devour as much Blanchard as early and often in your journey as you can.

If you are looking for books specifically about the hospitality business, I would recommend two; *Setting the Table* by Danny Meyer, and *Creating Magic* by Lee Cockerell. In terms of books that influenced the language I use to clarify principles of hospitality for people I am training, these two are at the top of the list. Both are very entertaining and interesting, and there are a ton of great tools in each for being better in all aspects of business.

Podcasts downloaded to your smart phone, tablet or PC are a great resource as well. For a while, I nearly stopped listening to anything in my car except podcasts as I drove to and from work—or anywhere else for that matter. I gobbled them up! My favorite, and I have mentioned it several times so far, is Manager Tools at http://www.manager-tools.com. As I progress in my career in leadership, Mike and Mark offer me more actionable advice than all of my past bosses combined. They also have created a really deep void in my soul too, as it has become dreadfully clear, that I have seldom had the benefit of working directly for such a leader. It makes me envious. And, it makes it harder in many ways to become that leader.

There are several cool things about Manager Tools. For one, most of their resources are free. They offer another collection of podcasts and resources titled Career Tools in which they offer tons of valuable guidance centered on advancing your career through a keener sense of professionalism.

You can also subscribe to their organization as a "licensee" for a relatively small fee. As a licensee, you gain access to some really powerful tools; notes from all of their shows, special cast series, résumé building and interviewing tips, and much more. Their casts are densely packed with information, they are entertaining, and they try (very successfully) to keep them under an hour. One of my favorite characteristics of their content, is that they bullet point all of the main points right at the beginning, so if you don't have time to listen to the whole cast, you can at least get the key points right away. Manager Tools is hands down the most powerful tool I have run across at this stage of my career, and their content has influenced me greatly.

It is important to learn how to hold people accountable, whether you are in a leadership role or not. The book I recommend beginning with for learning to hold people accountable to standards is Crucial Accountability, by Patterson,

Grenny, McMillan, Switzler, and Maxfield. This book really does a great job of giving you tools to hold people accountable to standards without beating them up. So often we do a good job of upholding our standards, but sometimes we forget that there are people on the other side of that.

Two more podcasts that I would recommend are The Dave Ramsey Show and The Andy Stanley Leadership Podcast.

Dave Ramsey is a financial guru and consumer advocate. His leadership is selfless, funny, compassionate, a touch hardnosed, and educational. If you struggle with building personal success financially, then Dave is a great resource to help get you on track.

Andy Stanley is new to me (less than a month at the time this book was published). His approach to leadership is very humble and patient. He makes no bones about sharing his mistakes and shortcomings, and the things that helped him overcome those. I have just gotten started on his series of casts, but what I have heard, I enjoy very much.

The last suggestion I would give you is to find a mentor. Look for someone that you respect that has achieved success in the areas where you want to improve. This could be a friend, relative or someone in your company. Approach them and ask to have a meeting to discuss your goals and ask them if they would be willing to meet with you periodically to discuss your ongoing development. This is a pretty big commitment, so you need to be 100% in, or you will end up wasting valuable time of yours, and of the person you are asking to mentor you.

I was lucky enough to have a professional executive coach work with me. If you can afford that, then I highly recommend it. A mentoring relationship can be a fantastic way to accelerate your knowledge, and ultimately your career.

Remember, it is super easy to get overwhelmed by all of the information you are absorbing. It gets easier, just relax and try not to take it all too literally—or, seriously. You are going to be getting advice and information from a thousand different angles at varying speeds. At first, just try different things. Keep the ones that work, adjust the ones that don't and try again. As you get more and more comfortable, pick up the pace. Have fun! Don't be afraid to fail, in fact, you should look forward to it.

You are a person. You are unique. Taking in all of the information you can from people who are more knowledgeable and experienced that you are can be an intimidating process. Make it yours. And, just remember that we all started out somewhere. Starting on this path has helped me become a better leader, a better husband, a better friend and a better father. I have learned a lot of valuable lessons along the way, and it has been a very exciting ride! Remember, you will only get out of it what you put in. If you are just going through the motions then you won't get far. And, the books that collect dust beside your bed aren't helping.

I will leave you with two sayings that I say to my kids:

Follow your dreams; the only ones who don't make it are the ones who give up.

And; Boys (or girls) without scars don't have any cool stories to tell.

Good luck on your journey, I wish you safe travels, and few roadblocks along the way.

For more information, or to contact the author, please visit our website at:

www.thehospitalityladder.com

or

www.facebook.com/thehospitalityladder